PREMIER Guides

Herefor
& the Wye Valley

Above: Hereford
Front cover: Bromyard
Back cover: River Wye at Hereford

Written by:Trevor Barrett

Photography: Lily Publications,
   Herefordshire Council & Chris Warren

First published
   by Lily Publications 2000

All accommodation advertised in this guide participates in the Wales Tourist Board's and ETC inspection scheme. If readers have any concern about the standards of any accommodation, please take the matter up directly with the provider of the accommodation, as soon as possible. Failing satisfaction, please contact the Wales Tourist Board, Development Services Unit, Brunel House, 2 Fitzalan Road, Cardiff CF2 1UY or Heart of England Tourist Board, Larkhill Road, Worcester, WR5 2EZ.
   Published by Lily Publications, PO Box 9, Narberth, Pembrokeshire, Wales SA68 0YT.
   Tel: (01834) 891461, Fax: (01834) 891463.

ISBN 1 899602 31 3

Contents

Welcome to Herefordshire 5

Farm & Countryside Attractions.................................8

Cider Country...11

Castles & Historic Sites..17

Parks & Gardens...22

Churches & Cathedrals..29

The Black & White Villages..37

Museums & Heritage Centres....................................43

Arts & Crafts..47

Hereford...50

A-Z of Herefordshire..63

Index...104

Maps

Herefordshire 64

Hereford 52

Bromyard 65

Coleford 72

Kington 78

Ledbury... 81

Leominster.. 86

Newent 90

Monmouth 90

Ross-on-Wye 96

Leominster

Welcome to Herefordshire

Best known for its rich farmland, white-faced cattle and extensive cider orchards, and largely untouched by industrial and urban development, Herefordshire is one of England's most rural and least spoilt counties.

It is here that many first-time visitors to Britain discover that the English countryside is everything and more they imagined it to be.

Centuries-old black and white half-timbered houses gather round charming village greens.

Ancient churches and forgotten hamlets nestle in the secluded isolation of leafy lanes and wooded hillsides.

Spawning salmon leap from the waters of the Wye as the river navigates a long and winding course through lush green meadows and spectacular gorges.

The narrow streets of market towns steeped in history and tradition carry busy shoppers about their business.

And at the centre of it all is the great cathedral city of Hereford, the gently beating heart of the county.

Yet Herefordshire was not always a picture of such rural tranquillity. This is border country, for centuries the scene of bloody battles between the English and the Welsh as well as major confrontations in the long-running Wars of the Roses and the Civil War. Defences such as the medieval fortress of Goodrich Castle and the even earlier earthworks of Offa's Dyke bear testimony to Herefordshire's troubled past.

For today's visitor this all adds up to a holiday experience packed with delights. From Hereford's magnificent 12th-century cathedral to the mouthwatering Tum Tum Trail and England's highest golf course, there is something here for everyone.

Activities

There are virtually endless opportunities to indulge in sports and leisure activities.

Herefordshire is an angler's paradise, the River Wye renowned for its salmon and the rivers Monnow, Lugg and Arrow for their trout.

There are 14 golf courses and 5 driving ranges.

Cycling, mountain biking, walking and horseriding are ideal ways to explore the superb countryside – or you can enjoy a bird's-eye view from a hot air balloon or helicopter at Shobdon.

And if you crave for even more excitement, try caving, canoeing, pot-holing, quad biking, whitewater rafting, climbing or paintball adventure games. Herefordshire is definitely not *all* peace and quiet!

Countryside attractions

Particularly popular with families and children are the county's farm and animal attractions, home to cuddly piglets, cute ponies and lots of other species large and small.

Cider has been a mainstay of the county's economy for hundreds of years, and the 9,500 acres of cider apple orchards now yield more than half of the UK's total annual cider production. Another successful Herefordshire speciality is perry, made from selected varieties of locally-grown pears. Visitors with a thirst for knowledge are invited to follow the Cider Route and uncork the full story for themselves.

Ross-on-Wye

A great variety of glorious gardens abounds in Herefordshire. More than ten National Collections can be found throughout the county, in addition to specialist nurseries, vineyards and the woodland nature reserve of Queenswood Country Park.

Food and hospitality

The home of Wye salmon, cider and Herefordshire beef has great culinary delights in store for visitors. Follow the Tum Tum Trail – a tour of local food producers – and discover exciting specialities such as leek and Little Hereford quiche, roast brown trout stuffed with cider apples and coated with Bodenham wine sauce, and damson and sloe gin ice cream with an autumn fruit compote.

You'll also find a wide choice of accommodation (including camping and caravan sites) and shortbreak holidays to choose from.

Golden Valley

The rich and fertile Golden Valley lies in the south-west of the county, between Hereford and the Black Mountains. Its name probably originates from a confusion by the Normans, who mistakenly translated the Welsh word for water (dwr) as the French word for golden (d'or). The valley is no less beautiful for that, and Dore is certainly a dominant name here. The River Dore, which rises in the Black Mountains, flows through the valley; at Abbey Dore stands the ruin of a large Early English church, part of a great 12th-century Cistercian abbey; and near Dorstone are the remains of Snodhill Castle, built to repel Welsh raiders who used the valley to cross the border and attack Norman estates.

Historical attractions

Herefordshire's turbulent past is recalled not only in historic houses and castle ruins, some of which are now owned by the National Trust and English Heritage, but also in a fascinating variety of museums and heritage centres. The county's proliferation of beautiful and unusual churches also provides great insight into the architecture and beliefs of centuries long gone. As for traditional arts and crafts, many of these live on and are well represented in galleries and workshops across the county.

Offa's Dyke

King Offa was ruler of Mercia, the most powerful of Britain's 8th-century kingdoms. He built the dyke on high ground east of the River Wye to deter intruders from crossing the water, and long stretches of the earthwork, up to 30 feet high, still survive between the Wye estuary and the Dee. Offa's Dyke Path is a long-distance National Trail from Chepstow to Prestatyn – a distance of 177 miles.

Royal Forest of Dean

Lying just outside the south-eastern corner of Herefordshire within very easy reach of Ross-on-Wye, the Royal Forest of Dean covers an area of more than 27,000 acres. In 1938 it was the first forest in Britain to be designated a National Forest Park, and is one of England's last remaining ancient forests. Long before this the Normans designated it a royal forest and it became a popular hunting ground for generations of monarchs. In more recent history it was exploited for its deposits of coal and iron ore and is still important for its timber. It is also a source of great recreational pursuits, notably walking, cycling, mountain biking and horseriding.

Shopping

The city of Hereford and the county's busy market towns offer visitors an excellent variety of shopping and places to eat. Hunting for antiques and collectables has never been more popular than it is today – and where better to start than Leominster, well established as the most important antiques centre in the region.

Towns and villages

Each of Herefordshire's historic market towns – Bromyard, Kington, Ledbury, Leominster and Ross-on-Wye – has a charm and character of its own. Then there are the wonderful black and white villages of Eardisland, Eardisley, Pembridge and Weobley. Located in the north-west of the county, they are famous for their timber-framed houses, cottages and inns, some of which date back as early as the 14th century and are a unique and very significant part of England's architectural heritage.

Wye Valley

An inspiration for Turner and Wordsworth alike, the unspoilt Wye Valley is designated an Area of Outstanding Natural Beauty. The Wye is also unique among England's rivers – the only one to be further designated a Site of Special Scientific Interest (SSSI) from source to mouth, which speaks volumes for the excellent water quality along its entire length.

The picturesque Wye Valley runs through Herefordshire for the best part of 70 miles between Hay-on-Wye and Monmouth, presenting wonderful views en route. The most impressive vantage point is Symond's Yat Rock – 504ft above sea level – where the river has cut a spectacular gorge into the limestone.

You can explore the Wye by boat or on foot. It is very popular for canoeing, kayaking, whitewater rafting, climbing, gorge walking and abseiling, not to mention the abundance of trout and salmon it offers to fishermen.

Hereford

7

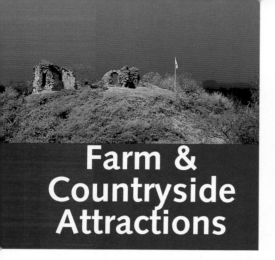

Farm & Countryside Attractions

Weobury

Broadgreen Open Farm Park, Madley
The farm is 7 miles south of Hereford and easily reached by bus. Attractions include friendly animals, tearooms, gift shop and educational centre. For further information ring 01981 250454.

Coddington Vineyard, near Ledbury
There is plenty to see and enjoy at this listed farmhouse and vineyard, including free wine tasting. For further information ring 01531 640668.

Cycleways
Cycling is an ideal way to explore and appreciate the wonderful countryside of Herefordshire's winding country lanes, rolling hills and rustic villages. In addition there are 4 designated cycleways to enjoy.
(1) *Hereford-Bishops Meadow Cycle Path*: Just a mile long, the path links the Great Western Railway to the city centre along the side of the River Wye.
(2) *Hereford-Great Western Way*: Here is a 2-mile route through the city of Hereford, following the disused trackbed of the Great Western Railway.
(3) *Ledbury*: This 1-mile cycle track was part of the former railway line through Ledbury. Access to it is from the car park in either the town centre or Leadon Picnic Place.

(4) *Ross-on-Wye* Utilising old railway trackbed on the outskirts of the town, this mile-and-a-half cycle route is accessible from the B4234 Walford road.

Frome Valley Vineyard, Bishops Frome
Here you can sample the wines and see various methods of growing and nurturing vines. For further information ring 01885 490735.

Hagley Court Vineyard, Hereford:
See page 57.

Hidden Highway
Explore the borderlands between England and Wales on a journey which begins at Ross-on-Wye, progresses through Herefordshire and Shropshire, and ends in Chester. En route you will see dramatic countryside and forgotten secret places that others rarely visit. A booklet describing the route in detail is available from any of Herefordshire's Tourist Information Centres.

Hop Trail

Follow the B4214 between Bromyard and Ledbury and in many of the surrounding fields you will see the varying stages of hop growing. You will also pass through the rustic villages of Bishops Frome and Castle Frome. For further information ring 01885 482341.

Lyne Down Farm & Cider

See page 16.

Malvern Hills & Herefordshire Beacon

Forming a natural divide between Worcestershire and Herefordshire, the Malverns were the source of much inspiration for composer Sir Edward Elgar, who wrote his two great symphonies here. He was born in 1857 at Upper Broadheath, near Worcester, and the house is a museum of his life and work.

Four miles south-west of the hillside town of Great Malvern is Herefordshire Beacon. This windy summit, 1,115 feet above sea level, was chosen by Iron Age dwellers as the site for a 32-acre hillfort, known as British Camp, the ramparts of which can still be seen. Built in approximately 200BC and one of the finest earthworks in Britain, the fortified settlement controlled a pass at the southern end of the Malvern Hills and supported a population of 2,000 people. Access to the beacon today is via a steep metalled path leading up from the car park – but the effort

is well rewarded with magnificent views.

The narrow rollercoaster ridge of the Malverns runs from north to south between the lowland vale of the River Severn and the Welsh borderland. From Great Malvern the hills stretch eight miles south, and the Herefordshire Beacon is one of six major summits.

Monkland Cheese Dairy, Leominster

See how 'Little Hereford' cheese is made by hand in the traditional method, and sample it in the farm shop. For further information ring 01568 720307.

National Snail Farming Centre, Credenhill

This display of wild British snails and snail farming includes recipes and a tour of the farm. For further information ring 01432 760218.

Newbridge Farm Park, near Ledbury

Situated at Little Marcle, this family attraction has indoor and outdoor play and picnic areas, farm walks and friendly animals to handle and feed. For further information ring 01531 670780.

Picnic sites

There 22 designated picnic sites in Herefordshire, in locations as varied, beautiful and fascinating as Bromyard Downs, Goodrich Castle and Ross Waterside. A full list is available from any of the county's Tourist Information Centres.

Pig Pen, Hareley Farm, Linley Green, near Whitbourne

This small family farm north-east of Bromyard specialises in pigs and is very much a working farm as well as an award-winning attraction. Conducted tours of the piggery present the chance to hold a piglet, and there are also lambs here in early spring. Other attractions include a woodland nature trail, play area, gift shop, home-made teas and plenty of space for picnics. For further information ring 01886 884362.

Queenswood Country Park
See page 26.

September Dairy Products, near Kington
Luxury ice cream in unusual and traditional flavours is produced at this working dairy farm at Almeley. For further information ring 01544 327561.

Shortwood Family Farm, Pencombe, near Bromyard
A very popular attraction for children, this busy working farm became organic on 1st May 2000. From 2.00pm every day the younger members of the family can help collect the eggs, milk the cow, feed the pigs and baby calves, cuddle the pets and chicks and (in dry weather) enjoy a trailer ride. And by seeing the cows milked by machine and fed by computer, they can also learn a great deal about how the farm is run. Other farm animals and attractions include shire horses, Shetland ponies, a farm trail, all-weather play barn and a tube slide. The last two weeks in October are devoted to making traditional cider. For further information ring 01885 400205.

The Small Breeds Farm Park & Owl Centre, near Kington
This award-winning family attraction has owls, waterfowl and a collection of miniature, rare and unusual animals. For further information ring 01544 231109.

Three Choirs Vineyard, near Ledbury
The second largest vineyard in England, Three Choirs is situated in beautiful countryside on the Ledbury-Newent road. For further information ring 01531 890555.

Walking
The diverse scenery of Herefordshire makes it a real treat for anyone who enjoys walking. There are walks to suit all tastes, the landscape ranging from the stark beauty and stunning views of the Malvern Hills to the tranquil Leadon Vale and the beautiful Wye Valley. Three are three long-distance footpaths to challenge serious walkers – Offa's Dyke Footpath (Chepstow-Prestatyn), Wye Valley Walk (Chepstow-Rhayader) and Mortimer Trail (Ludlow-Kington).

Border Trails
Explore the Marches at your own pace, by car, foot or bike, with a choice of trails. For further information ring Upper Newton Farmhouse, Kinnersley on 01544 327710.

Westons Cider
See page 16.

Wobage Farm Craft Workshops, Upton Bishop
See page 49.

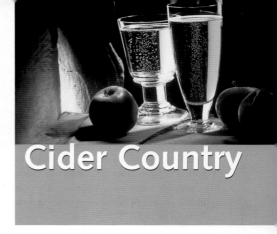

Cider Country

The history of cidermaking can be traced back a thousand years and more. Little has changed in the cidermaking process, other than the scale of production and the advent of modern machines to replace the heavy stone wheel which crushed the apples and the manual screw presses which extracted the juice.

Herefordshire has been the major centre of cidermaking in Britain for the last 350 years. As an agricultural industry it has several unique attractions, especially in times of depression. For one thing, cider fruit keeps, and its size and appearance are not important. For another, cider production occupies the slack months at the year end. And then there are the orchards themselves, which are useful for grazing animals and other purposes.

The story of cidermaking in Herefordshire also reflects the tradition of farmers producing cider for consumption during the following year by the farm workers, as well as selling it to local pubs and cider merchants.

The process for producing cider can be divided into three key stages – harvesting the fruit, milling and pressing the apples, and fermentation.

In spring the cider apple orchards of Herefordshire burst into blossom. By autumn the trees are laden with fruit and the harvest begins, taking place from mid-September through to Christmas. The specially-grown varieties of cider apples are stored in mounds or *tumps* and become *daddicky* – somewhere past over-ripe.

Extracting the juice from cider apples, which are very hard, requires the two stages of milling and pressing. Milling crushes the apples into a pulp, and the juice from this is then pressed out and put into large casks which traditionally hold between 60 and 120 gallons.

The yeast in the apples now begins the process of fermentation, evident by the fact that the juice begins to *fret* – meaning to hiss or sing a little. Initial fermentation takes about six weeks, after which a wooden bung is hammered into each cask to seal it and prevent air from getting in. The cider then matures for several months.

The next and final stage is to blend the cider to produce the wide variety of styles so familiar today – dry, sweet, still and sparkling.

Cider trivia

❏ There are already 9,500 acres of cider orchards in Herefordshire, and the figure is growing annually by more than 600 acres.

Harvesting the Apples

❑ Approximately 6.3 million gallons of cider are made in Herefordshire every year – well over half of the UK's total annual production.

❑ It was traditional in Herefordshire to pay part of a farm labourer's wages in cider. This practice was so popular that it continued on many farms even after it was made illegal in 1887.

❑ There are as many as 500 small cider producers in the county. It is legal to make up to 1,500 gallons a year without paying excise duty.

❑ In 1667 the vicar of Dilwyn reported that parishioners who lived to ages ranging from between 90 to 114 had drunk nothing but cider. He also claimed that a morris dance had been performed by ten people who combined ages amounted to more than a thousand years!

❑ It is customary on the eve of Twelfth Night to wassail the orchards to ensure next year's crop. Fires are usually lit – one in the middle of a circle of twelve small ones.

❑ The earliest written mention of cider can be found in the Wycliffite 'Cider' Bible, written in the 15th century and now housed in the Chained Library in Hereford Cathedral.

❑ Although not as well known as cider, Herefordshire perry is another drink traditionally produced in the county, particularly around the Herefordshire-Gloucestershire border. It is made from perry pears, of which there are at least 120 varieties – some with outrageously appropriate names such as Dead Boy, Mumblehead and Merrylegs!

Apples ready for pressing

Herefordshire Cider Route
The best way to explore the county's cider country is to follow this circular trail. Beginning in Hereford at the Cider Museum and King Offa Distillery, and the adjacent Bulmers Cider Mill, the route takes you in a clockwork direction to seven other attractions, ranging from farmhouse cidermakers to a specialist cider retailer. They are Dunkertons Cider Mill (Pembridge), Orchard, Hive and Vine (Leominster), Franklins Cider Farm Shop (Little Hereford, close to the borders of Worcestershire and Shropshire), Knights Cider (Storridge, near Malvern), Westons Cider (Much Marcle), Lyne Down Farm (Much Marcle) and Broome Farm (Peterstow, Ross-on-Wye). Full details are given in the leaflet *Herefordshire Cider Route*, available free from the county's Tourist Information Centres.

Broome Farm, Ross-on-Wye
Traditional farmhouse cider has been produced here since the early 1980's, and the farm has won several prestigious awards.

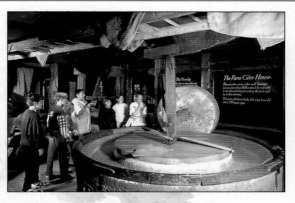

CIDER MUSEUM &
KING OFFA DISTILLERY
HEREFORD

Directions
The Cider Museum is situated west of Hereford off the A438 Hereford to Brecon Road

In the heart of Herefordshire, the Cider Museum explores the history of traditional cider making worldwide. Visit the reconstructed farm ciderhouse, the champagne Cider cellars, the Vat house. and the Cooper's Workshop. See the Herefordshire 'Pomonas' - beautiful books dating from the 19th Century which illustrate the varieties of cider apples and perry pears grown from earliest times to the present day.

King Offa Cider Brandy is distilled on the premises and you can try free samples of distillery products in the Museum Gift Shop.

Programme of temporary exhibitions and special events throughout the year, including the annual Cider & Perrymaking Competition in May and the Cidermaking Festival in October.

Free car and coach parking.

The Pomona Tea Room is open from April to October and at other times by arrangement. Special admission rates for pre-booked parties of 15 or more.

Admission Charges (from April 2000)

Adults	£2.40
Concessions (children, OAP's, students)	£1.90

Special rates for pre-booked parties of 15 or more:

Adults	£1.90
Concessions	£1.40

For further details Tel: (01432) 354207

Bulmers

THE CIDER EXPERIENCE....IN HEREFORD

The historic city of Hereford on the banks of the River Wye is world famous for its cider. They were making cider here long before they built the cathedral over a thousand years ago.

For well over a century the city has been the home of Bulmers, the best known of all cider makers, and the cider mill is just a few minutes walk from the city centre.

"The Cider Experience" offered by Bulmers includes a visit to the Cider Museum to see the drink's heritage and a tour of the modern cider mill, ending up with a popular cider tasting session.

Tours are by appointment only and cost £3.95 or £2.95 for pensioners.

If you are on holiday and want to join a tour telephone to check availability.

For further details or to book a visit please write or telephone the Visitors Centre

**HP Bulmer Limited,
The Cider Mills,
Plough Lane,
Hereford HR4 0LE**

**Telephone:
01432 352000**

A new addition to the range is prize-winning Broome Farm Perry. Cream teas are available here. For further information ring 01989 769556 or 562824.

Bulmers Visitors Centre & Cider Mill, Hereford

Founded in Hereford in 1887 by Percy Bulmer, son of a local vicar, HP Bulmer Limited is now the world's leading cider producer. Here at the Visitors Centre and Cider Mill in Plough Lane, just a 5-minute walk from the city's cathedral, you can join an organised tour to learn something of the heritage and traditions of cider making, and see such famous Bulmers brands as Strongbow and Woodpecker being made. Better still, you also get to taste them!

The way in which cider is made at the mill is highly automated, in sharp contrast to the more traditional methods still used by other cider producers in the county. The guided tour begins at the Bulmers Visitors Centre, created in the vaulted cellars beneath Percy's original mill in Ryelands Street (which is now the Cider Museum). After a short introductory film you will see the silos, where the cider apples arrive at harvest time, and the press hall. Then it's on to the huge steel fermentation vessels, the bottling hall, the keg filling plant and back to the Visitors Centre for free tastings. The tour takes about two and a half hours, and there is also time to pick up momentos in the Visitors Shop.

Bulmers' commitment to maintaining the traditional English cider apple, which is grown mostly in Herefordshire, can be measured by the fact that in recent years the company has joined forces with local farmers to plant a further 4,500 acres of cider orchards. In the autumn you can see the apples being delivered; the mill presses up to 100,000 tonnes of cider fruit a season to keep pace with the growing demand for cider both in Britain and overseas.

Orchards in Spring

To join an organised tour you must book in advance, though casual visitors can be accommodated if places are available. For further information, including booking, ring 01432 352000.

Cider Museum & King Offa Distillery, Hereford

The only registered museum in the UK devoted entirely to the making of cider and perry, this unique visitor attraction in Hereford tells the story of traditional cidermaking around the world. The King Offa Distillery is a working exhibit, granted the first licence to distil cider in this country for more than 200 years, and it produces cider brandy, apple aperitif and cider liqueur. The whole process of cidermaking is revealed here, from harvesting, milling, pressing, fermentation and blending. Other attractions include champagne cider cellars, 19th-century bottling equipment, free tastings, gift shop, off licence and tea rooms. For further information ring 01432 354207.

Dunkertons Cider Mill & Restaurant, Pembridge

See the mill, taste traditional cider and satisfy your appetite in the bar and restaurant. For further information ring 01544 388653.

Franklins Cider Farm Shop, Little Hereford, Shropshire

On the northern borders of Herefordshire on the banks of the River Teme, the farm produces traditional ciders and perries in sweet, medium and dry. The Cider Farm Shop also sells a wide selection of other country produce such as honey, jams, preserves and wines. For further information ring 01584 810488.

Knights Cider, Storridge, near Malvern

Established in 1973, this family-run business produces traditional cider and has won many awards in the process. The orchards extend to over 200 acres and a footpath runs from the shop and joins the Worcestershire Way. For further information ring 01684 574594.

Lyne Down Cider, Much Marcle

Small-scale traditional cidermaking is demonstrated here during the making season, so it is best to telephone first on 01531 660691 to avoid disappointment.

Orchard, Hive and Vine, Leominster

This retail outlet specialises in local ciders and perry, apple juice, mead, local wines and beers. For further information ring 01568 611232.

Westons Cider, Much Marcle, near Ledbury

Situated amongst cider apple and perry pear orchards, this family-run business was established in the old village of Much Marcle in 1880 by Henry Weston. The original stone mill and screw press which he used were eventually retired to the farmhouse garden, and are still there. Today the company remains independent and produces a wide range of renowned ciders and perries, as well as welcoming visitors for tours of the Westons Cider Mill, which is open all year round. The tour takes up to 75 minutes and includes a tasting of ciders and perries in the Visitors Centre and Shop. A further attraction is The Scrumpy House Restaurant. Delightfully set in a converted 17th-century barn, it serves morning coffees, lunches, afternoon teas and evening meals, and caters for private parties.

For further information on Westons Cider, including tour bookings, ring 01531 660233. To book at The Scrumpy House Restaurant ring 01531 660626.

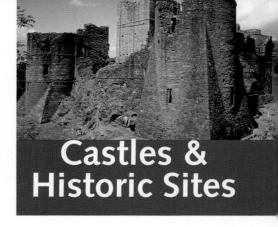

Castles & Historic Sites

Herefordshire's long, eventful and often bloody history, particularly in the Welsh Marches, is reflected in the number of ruins, ancient sites, properties and estates open for public viewing – many of them in the care of either the National Trust or English Heritage. The following is a brief guide to how a visit to the county can take you back to the days of Normans, Saxons, Romans and before.

Arthur's Stone, Dorstone
The remains of this Neolithic chambered tomb are in the care of English Heritage. The tomb is set on a ridge about a mile from Dorstone church and it belongs to the group of chambered long barrows known as the Cotswold type. According to legend this is the tomb of King Arthur or of a giant killed by him.

Berrington Hall, near Leominster
Built in the late 18th century, this elegant house with a richly decorated interior and gardens created by Capability Brown is now in the care of the National Trust. For further information ring 01568 615721.

Burton Court, Eardisland
Standing about a mile south of the village, this mansion has a great hall dating from medieval times. The hall now forms part of a house which is mainly late 18th century, but it also boasts a Tudor-style facade built in 1912 by Sir Clough William-Ellis, who created the Italianate fantasy village of Portmeirion on the Cardigan Bay coastline in Wales. Also of interest to visitors is Burton Court's extensive collection of European and Oriental costumes and curios. For further information ring 01544 388231.

Capler Camp, near Fownhope
A mile south-east of Fownhope, this twin rampart Iron Age hillfort stands above the River Wye.

Clifford Castle
The remains of this 11th-century castle at Clifford comprise gatehouse, hall and round towers. For further information ring 01497 831798.

Croft Ambrey, near Leominster
This Iron Age hillfort is set in a commanding position on a limestone ridge about a mile to the north of the present Croft Castle, with views over much of Wales. It stands within the 1,350-acre estate now owned by the National Trust. For further information ring 01568 780246.

Clifford Castle

17

Croft Castle, near Leominster

The castle estate is owned by the National but is still occupied by the Croft family, who have lived here almost continuously since Norman times. The castle, 5 miles north of Leominster, stands in ancient parkland and woods and is an impressive mixture of battlements and country house, the 18th-century interior housed within walls and towers dating from the 14th and 15th centuries. For further information ring 01568 780246.

Dinedor Camp

This large hillfort stands on Dinedor Hill, 3 miles south-east of Hereford. It offers pleasant walking and extensive views across the city.

Eastnor Castle

It is easy to believe that this fairytale castle has graced the landscape for many centuries, but in fact it was built in 1812 – the dream of the first Earl Somers, who commissioned the young architect Robert Smirke to create the magnificent baronial home we see today.

Less than three miles east of Ledbury in the foothills of the Malverns, it is a superb example of the great Norman and Gothic revival of the medieval fortress. Eastnor Castle, now the home of its owners the Hervey-Bathurst family, stands in a dramatic setting that embraces a deer park, an arboretum and a lake, and the interior is lavishly decorated in a display of Italianate and Gothic splendour.

The interior, showing many of the castle's treasures, is as impressive as the exterior, a series of state rooms leading off the vast 60ft hall. The spectacular Gothic drawing room, designed by Pugin, still has much of the original furniture and, along with the Octagon Saloon and the Long Library, enjoys wonderful views over the lawned terraces to the lake and Malvern Hills beyond. In the library is a prized collection of books and tapestries decorated in the style of the Italian Renaissance. Many other rooms are open to visitors, including the grand dining room.

The 5,000-acre estate, much of it farmed, also has a great deal worth seeing. The deer park, with a herd of about 200 red deer, is a designated SSSI (Site of Special Scientific Interest). An arboretum of rare trees descends to the 22-acre lake, and on a fine day there is no better setting in which to enjoy a picnic.

Eastnor Castle's many other visitor attractions include an adventure playground, garden centre, children's maze, lakeside and woodland walks, a gift shop and a tea room. For further information ring 01531 633160.

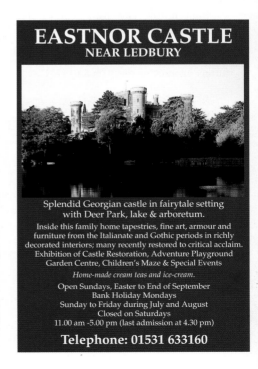

Goodrich Castle

Rising dramatically from a jagged slab of rock on which it is founded, 4 miles south-west of Ross-on-Wye, this English Heritage monument is the only Norman stronghold in the county and the best preserved of all Herefordshire's castles.

The imposing ruins of Goodrich Castle perch spectacularly on a high wooded hill overlooking the River Wye – an impressive moated fortress dating back to the 12th century, built as a defence against Welsh raiders.

Constructed from red sandstone, it has a grey sandstone 12th-century keep, below which is a dungeon, and extensive remains of 13th-century walls. The castle was the home of the Talbot family – Earls of Shrewsbury – but when it passed by marriage to the Earls of Kent in the early 17th century it was no longer inhabited. The final fall from grace came in the Civil War. After an unsuccessful siege it was destroyed by Cromwellian troops, the damage inflicted by a 200-pounder cannon known as Roaring Meg, which is now on display at Churchill House Museum in Hereford.

The views over the surrounding countryside and meandering River Wye are breathtaking. So too are those from the famous tall rock of Symonds Yat, which is within easy driving distance. For further information on Goodrich Castle ring 01600 890538.

Hellens

Set in fifteen acres with coppices, lawns and fish ponds, this home dates from 1292 and is one of the oldest in England. Notable features include a pigeon house of 1641 and a collection of old carriages. Guided tours are available but telephone first for opening times on 01531 660668.

Eastnor Castle

Herefordshire Beacon

The remains of a large Iron Age hillfort stand on the summit of the beacon, which is on the long narrow ridge of the Malvern Hills. For more information see page 9.

Longtown Castle, near Abbeydore

In the care of English Heritage, the ruins of this 12th-century castle give magnificent views across the valley of the River Monnow to the Black Mountains. The castle has an unusual cylindrical keep, most often found in Wales and the Marches, and the castle walls are fifteen feet thick.

Lower Brockhampton

A fascinating National Trust property, this late 14th-century half-timbered manor house is set in more than 1700 acres and features a very unusual 15th-century gatehouse straddling the moat. Other points of interest include the medieval hall, screens passage, parlour, minstrels' gallery, the ruins of a 12th-century chapel, woodland walks

Clifford Castle

and a sculpture trail. For further information ring 01885 488099.

Moccas Court

Standing on the banks of the River Wye in parkland laid out by Capability Brown, this Georgian country house and estate is 12 miles west of Hereford. It was designed by John Nash and Robert Adam and presents a series of fine ground-floor rooms to visitors. For further information ring 01981 500381.

Snodhill Castle, near Dorstone

The ruins of the castle stand a mile south-east of Dorstone, the 12th-century keep being of particular interest.

Goodrich Castle

Parks & Gardens

Abbey Dore Court Garden

This rambling, semi-formal six-acre garden is intersected by the River Dore. For further information ring 01981 240419.

Arrow Cottage Garden, Near Weobley

Carefully maintained, this stylish garden is complemented by an attractive tea room. For further information ring 01544 318468.

Bringsty Herbs

Over 300 varieties of herbs and rockery and cottage garden plants are on display here. For further information ring 01886 821482.

Broadfield Court Gardens & Vineyard, Bodenham

Here you will find five acres of Elizabethan gardens and vineyards set in glorious countryside. For further information ring 01568 797483.

Bryan's Ground Edwardian Garden, near Presteigne

There are numerous attractions at this beautiful three-acre garden – colour-themed garden rooms, parterres, topiary, Gothic garden, and kitchen and herb gardens. For further information ring 01544 260001.

The Garden at the Bannut, Bringsty, near Bromyard

A striking combination of formal and informal gardens are to be found in this superb countryside setting less than three miles east of Bromyard. Covering an area of two and a half acres, the attractions include lawns, mixed borders, island beds, heather gardens, informal walks through interesting trees and shrubs, and an unusual knot garden. There are also lovely views to the Malvern Hills, and most of the garden is accessible to disabled visitors. For further information ring 01885 482206.

Hergest Croft Gardens, Kington

Lying in the heart of the Welsh Marches, with stunning views over the Black Mountains, the gardens have been a century in the making and cover more than fifty acres. The four distinct gardens have over 4,000 rare shrubs and trees and a great variety of features, from hidden valleys, woodland glades and open parkland to gorgeous flower borders and

Bannut Gardens

HERGEST CROFT GARDENS

Situated in the heart of the Welsh marches with stunning views towards the black mountains. Created over 100 years by three generations of the Banks family, there are hidden valleys, woodland glades, open parkland, gorgeous flower borders and striking autumn colour.
The Gardens are open daily from April 1st to October 31st 1.30pm - 6.00pm. Pre booked groups and season ticket holders are welcome outside regular hours throughout the year. Free car parking. Dogs on leads permitted.

The Hergest Estate Office, Kington, Herefordshire HR5 3EG
Tel/Fax: (01544) 230160
email: banks@hergest.kc3.co.uk
website: www.hergest.co.uk

striking autumn colours. The gardens open daily from 1st April till the end of October and disabled visitors are welcome. For further information ring 01544 230160.

How Caple Court Gardens

Overlooking the River Wye at How Caple, these 11-acre Edwardian gardens offer excellent walks and other attractions. For further information ring 01989 740626.

Kenchester Water Gardens, Hereford

These gardens are home to the national water lily collection, as well as an extensive range of tropical cold water and marine fish. For further information ring 01432 270981.

Lingen Nursery and Garden, near Bucknell, Shropshire

Celebrating its twenty-first year in 2000, Lingen Nursery and Garden is the pride and joy of horticulturalist Kim Davis and his wife Maggie. Open every day from February to October, these glorious gardens at Lingen in the Welsh Marches, between Presteigne and Bucknell, have gained a national reputation for their rare alpine and herbaceous plants, many of which are not readily available elsewhere in the country. The stock and display plants are housed in a variety of settings which extend to two acres, and also under development is the Far Field Garden, covering a similar area and incorporating a large rock outcrop, bog garden and island beds. There is plenty of colour and variety to be seen throughout the year, including two national collections held at Lingen under the NCCPG collections

LINGEN NURSERY AND GARDEN

*Extensively planted gardens
* Specialist alpine and herbaceous nursery
* National collections of Iris Sibirica and Herbaceous Campanula
* Personal collections of Auricula, Primula and penstemons
* Tea room
* Access to Mortimer trail

H.E.T.B. QUALITY ASSURED VISITOR ATTRACTION
LINGEN NURSERY AND GARDEN
LINGEN, NR. BUCKNELL,
SHROPSHIRE SY7 0DY
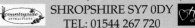
TEL: 01544 267 720
email: kim&maggie@lingen.freeserve.co.uk
Brown tourist signs off A4113 and B4362

scheme, and guided tours and talks are also available, tailored to the interests of each individual group. A further attraction is that Lingen is located on the loop of the Mortimer Trail, which runs from Kington to Ludlow, and so makes for a full and fascinating day out in superb countryside. For further information ring 01544 267720.

Overcroft Garden Nursery, Hereford
Overcourt is a specialist nursery growing a wide range of herbaceous perennials. For further information ring 01432 880845.

Pentwyn Cottage Garden,
near Bacton
Enjoy this tranquil mature garden with its colourful borders. For further information ring 01981 240508.

Burford House Gardens

Period Plants, Weston-under-Penyard
Old-fashioned historical plants can be bought here. For further information ring 01989 565422.

The Picton Garden,
Colwall, Near Malvern
Open for the National Gardens Scheme, the garden enjoys a beautiful setting on the western slopes of the Malvern Hills and is home to the national Michaelmas Daisy collection. There are moderate gravel paths throughout the garden and disabled visitors are welcome. For opening times and further information ring 01684 540416.

Queenswood Country Park,
Dinmore Hill, near Leominster
Comprising 170 acres, this wonderful woodland nature reserve is a delightful mix of attractive parkland and a 67-acre arboretum containing more than 450 rare

and exotic trees. Apart from the superb hilltop views, the many attractions include waymarked paths and nature trails, picnic and play areas, a licensed cafe in a restored timber-framed building, and a gift shop and Tourist Information Centre. The park is open every day from dawn till dusk and is signposted midway between Hereford and Leominster on the A49. It is also well served by buses. For further information ring 01568 797052.

Stockton Bury Gardens, Kimbolton, near Leominster

Stockton Bury is a traditional mixed farm with a history dating back to the 7th century. The cultivated garden, part of an orchard where cider apples are grown, covers an area of approximately four acres, divided into several fascinating areas which include a Kitchen Garden, Pool Garden, Pigeon House Garden and a

Stockton Bury Gardens

Secret Garden. The latter lies adjacent to The Dingle – an area which was formerly an old quarry and is now being developed as an area of wild woodland. The garden enjoys a superb setting and spectacular views of the Black Mountains. For further information ring 01568 613432.

The Amazing Hedge Puzzle, Symonds Yat West

Since the maze was planted 21 years ago, thousands of visitors from around the world have been attracted here. For further information about the Jubilee Maze and Museum of Mazes, ring 01600 890360.

Weir Garden, near Hereford

The National Trust owns this garden along the banks of the River Wye, which is designated a Site of Special Scientific Interest (SSSI). For further information ring 01684 850051.

The Van Kampen Gardens at Hampton Court, Hope Under Dinmore

In June 2000 the stunning new Van Kampen Gardens open for visitors – a creation that's fascinating both in terms of its sheer scale and for its unique combination of innovative features and garden schemes reminiscent of past styles.

The 1,000-acre estate was founded in 1430 as a reward for a knight's bravery at Agincourt, and it became famous throughout Europe in the 17th and 18th centuries for its fabulous formal gardens. The late medieval house and 25 acres of parkland and gardens had been sadly neglected in recent years, but in 1994 the estate was purchased by the Van Kampen family – and their commitment has given Hampton Court Herefordshire a new lease of life.

The garden project is very much a work in progress, but the transformation is well underway. New features include the extension of the original Haha, which now commands impressive views of the reinstated lake and new gatehouse; a yew maze with a folly at its centre hiding the entrance to a tunnel that leads to a hermit's grotto and sunken garden with a pool and waterfalls; parterres and pavilions; a unique garden water system, naturally powered by a waterwheel supplying the garden's many water features, canals and waterfalls; and a rose garden with a beautifully-sculpted birdbath, continually replenished by the water system. Both the kitchen gardens and the ornamental gardens are managed organically.

The gardens are being built almost entirely by the estate's own employees, many of whom live on the estate. The groundsmen have come in to assist with the large landscaping operations, the team of gardeners is developing and implementing planting plans, and highly-skilled masons and carpenters – initially employed to carry out estoration work on the house– have been set to work forming the garden buildings and water features.

The work on this extraordinary project started in 1996 and is still far from completion. The designers, gardeners and craftsmen still have many more

Eardisland

fascinating creations to unveil. These include the organic kitchen garden, the restoration of the Joseph Paxton-designed conservatory , and the construction of a 32-metre-span wooden footbridge over the River Lugg.

Hampton Court Herefordshire is located on the A417 at Hope Under Dinmore, just off the A49 between Leominster and Hereford. The village is well served by local buses. For further information ring 01568 797777.

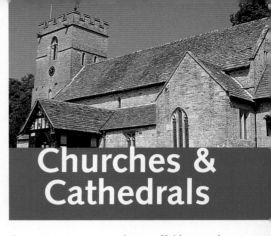

Churches & Cathedrals

Churches in England have always been the centre of rural communities, and Christianity goes back a long way in Herefordshire.

Wooden churches dedicated to long-forgotten Celtic saints once stood at many of the sites where stone buildings exist today. Timber was an abundant local resource, and there is little evidence that stone was used to build churches much before the middle of the 11th century.

When the Normans arrived they ignored and abandoned local tradition and rebuilt and rededicated many churches. Most that we see today in the county were built by 1200, but medieval builders were keen to display the latest architectural style and there was much rebuilding in the late 13th and early 14th centuries. This is evident from larger windows and pointed arches.

The hard physical task of building the churches – quarrying the stone, moving it to

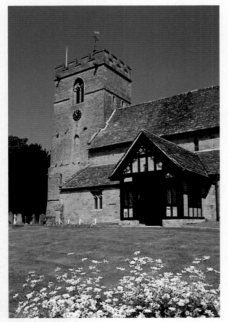

Lyonshall Church

the site, erecting wooden scaffolding and laying the courses – was carried out by local people. Axes were used to shape the stone, and it was not until the chisel became more widely used in the latter part of the 12th century that the decorative Romanesque zigzag and chevron designs really came into their own. Remarkably, several decades before this a workshop of highly skilled stone carvers was creating beautiful pictures during the construction of several churches in the county. Today these craftsmen are referred to as the Herefordshire School of Romanesque Sculpture, and examples of their incredible work can be seen at several churches, most notably Kilpeck.

Wood also lends interesting features to the county's churches. It figures particularly in roof construction, and in many cases the roof timbers are exposed and reveal the technique used by the builders. Church furnishings were also made from wood, such as screens, communion tails, lecterns, pulpits and altar tables.

Always of interest are towers and spires – often very familiar features in the landscape. They come in a great variety of shapes and sizes and are built in wood, stone and even fibreglass! Herefordshire is of special interest because seven village churches in the county have detached bell towers, the finest example being Pembridge.

Stained glass windows first appeared in England in the 12th century, but early glass was not of great quality and very little of it

Weobley

VI
VII
VIII
IX
X
XI
XII
I
II
III
IIII
V

ONE DAY TELLETH ANOTHER, AND·
ONE NIGHT CERTIFIETH ANOTHER

remains. In Herefordshire there are excellent examples from the 14th century – notably Eaton Bishop – when the art of stained glass developed at a pace.

Many Herefordshire churches are made from sandstone. This creates problems for the highly skilled craftsmen of today who carry out repairs and restoration work, since sandstone is difficult to clean, suffers badly from the effects of weathering and is not in great supply.

The following is a guide to some of the most interesting churches in the county, but there are many others. It goes without saying that Hereford Cathedral is a must for any visitor, while the historic cathedrals of Worcester and Gloucester are also within easy reach.

Abbey Dore

As with all Cistercian monasteries, Abbey Dore is dedicated to St Mary. The monks have long since gone and the abbey is now a parish church, standing in a secluded place in the Golden Valley and displaying a wealth of interesting features, including stonework, wood carvings and wall paintings.

Allensmore

Set by a farmyard and dedicated to St Andrew, Allensmore's church is notable for its medieval glass and as the location of the infamous Herefordshire Commotion of 1605 – an event that shocked religious leaders of the day.

Bishop's Frome

The massive font of St Mary's is more than 700 years old. The church stands near hop yards and orchards in the centre of the village, and outstanding features include a handsome lychgate, 19th-century porch and 12th-century Norman doorway and chancel.

Pembridge

Brampton Abbots

The nave and chancel of St Michael's reveal the church's Norman origins, and there is interesting stonework in the south doorway. The chancel arch and south porch date from the 14th century. Interesting internal features include a restored Perpendicular font and bowl of the piscina, rediscovered in 1857.

Bredwardine

The diarist Francis Kilvert, rector of the church for the last two years of his life, is buried here. The church was built soon after the conquest of 1066 and the nave still has its Norman windows and doors. There might also have been a Norman central tower; the present

The tower dates from the Georgian period. There is an effigy of local knight Sir Robert Vaughan, who died at Agincourt.

Brockhampton

All Saints' in Brockhampton is one of only three thatched churches in the country, and has a very unusual design that combines traditional crafts with exceptional workmanship. There are excellent examples of work produced here by the finest arts and crafts scholars. Among them are stained glass from Christopher Whall, wood carving by George Jack and two unique tapestries designed by Edward Burne-Jones and made by the William Morris workshops.

Bromyard

Cruciform in shape, St Peter's has a massive 14th-century central tower with an unusual corner stair turret. The east window contains modern glass and depicts saints, prophets, martyrs and Hereford Cathedral.

Eardisland

The picturesque village of Eardisland is dominated by the great tower of the church, which houses a peal of eight bells. The church dates from the 13th century but much of it was rebuilt in 1864. Every year a major photographic exhibition is presented here. For information on the exhibition currently showing ring 01568 708255.

Eaton Bishop

Dedicated to St Michael and All Angels, the church is renowned for its early stained glass, which dates from c1330.

Fownhope

The parish church of St Mary is one of the county's largest churches. Its most interesting architectural features span several periods – Norman, Early English, Decorated and Perpendicular. The long nave has an oak trussed roof from the 15th and 16th centuries, and the central tower is Norman, as is the 12th-century tympanum – one of the finest examples in England. The chancel was rebuilt in the 13th century. The

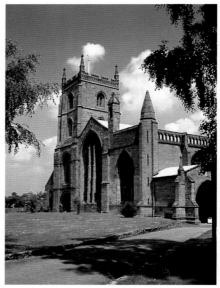

Leominster Priory

church also has a massive early 14th-century oak chest.

Foy

St Mary's at Foy is the third church to stand on this site. It dates from the 14th century, though the north doorway and chancel window are survivors from its predecessor. The pulpit, screen, communion rail and stalls all display very good examples of 17th-century woodwork, and the ten-sided font has the largest bowl of any of the county's churches.

Goodrich

The church of St Giles enjoys an elevated setting and is close to the village and the magnificent ruins of Goodrich Castle. The internal north arcade was built in two stages in the 13th and 14th centuries. Also dating from the 14th century are the west tower, broach spire and south porch, the east window being a creation of the 15th century.

Hereford

All Saints

Standing in High Street, this medieval building is striking for its 240-ft tower. The interior, now transformed into a meeting place complete with cafe, boasts great timber roofs, many examples of medieval craftsmanship and fine 20th-century glass.

Belmont Abbey

Designed by Pugin, whose work can also be seen at Eastnor Castle, this Benedictine abbey was built between 1854 and 1857 as a Roman Catholic cathedral. It became an abbey in 1920 and is now also a parish church. Belmont has many outstanding architectural features and adjoining monastic gardens, and visitors are welcome.

Hereford Cathedral

Cathedral buildings have stood on this site since Saxon times, and the present structure dates from 1140 and displays architectural styles which span the centuries from Norman times to the 1990's. For further information see page 57.

How Caple

Dating from the early 13th century, the church of St Andrew and St Mary has many interesting features. The 14th-century chancel has a later low pitched oak roof with bosses, and the west tower nave and south transept are from the late 17th century. The wealth of internal features includes the diptych on the north wall, believed to be German and early 16th century; an unusual screen carved by Grinling Gibbons; late Norman font; Jacobean pulpit; and good examples of modern windows.

Kilpeck

Kilpeck, 8 miles south-west of Hereford, has been described as one of the most remarkable little churches in Britain – and with full justification. A Norman church displaying excellent examples of the Herefordshire School of Sculpture, it boasts a wealth of wonderful rare carvings in red sandstone. It is dedicated to St Mary and St David and has changed little since it was built in 1136, the sandstone miraculously defying the ravages of time and remaining in near-perfect condition. The south doorway and west windows are particularly outstanding. Beside the church are earthworks – all that remains of a Norman castle.

Kington

The massive detached Norman tower at St Mary's was built in around 1200, and the church itself came later. The 13th-century chancel has fine lancet windows with stained glass of the same period. In the chapel is the tomb of Sir Thomas Vaughan, who died at the Battle of Banbury in 1469.

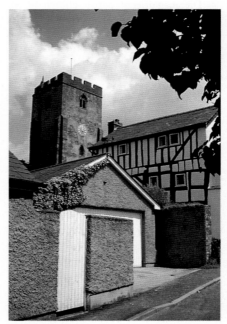

Leintwardine

33

Peterchurch

Ledbury

The magnificent parish church of St Michael and All Angels has been the centre of worship in Ledbury for more than eight centuries. It is rich with treasures and memorials from across the ages. The detached tower was built in the 13th century, the spire and embattled belfry being added in 1723.

Leintwardine

Dedicated to St Mary Magdalene and dominating this area of the Teme Valley, this fine medieval church is built on the site of a Roman vallum and is often referred to as 'the cathedral of north Herefordshire'. The stalls with misericords reputedly came from Wigmore Abbey after its dissolution.

Leominster

Leominster's Benedictine Priory was founded in 1123, succeeding an earlier nunnery, and up until its dissolution in 1539 it was home to a community of monks attached to the royal monastery at Reading.

All that remains of the monastic church are the two naves and the south aisle. Features of note are fine tracery in the windows and intricate carving on the remaining Norman capitals.

Madley

Reputed to be the birthplace of St Dubricious, Madley has been a place of pilgrimage for 1400 years. The church is one of the region's finest, containing treasures such as medieval wall paintings, stained glass and choir stalls. The tower and crypt are open by arrangement.

Pembridge

The 14th-century church of St Mary in Pembridge has a remarkable detached bell tower – the finest of the seven detached towers in Herefordshire. Made of timber, it houses a peel of five bells. The church stands in an elevated position and is approached by steep steps from the village. The door still has its original 14th-century hinges, and local legend has it that the leathery substance underneath the sanctuary knocker is skin of a marauding Viking.

Peterchurch

According to legend, St Peter – to whom this 12th-century church is dedicated – might have passed through here on his way to Rome, though it is more likely that the site has Saxon origins and dates back to the 8th century and the reign of King Offa. The church is unique in having four sections with a double chancel, and the spire is a modern 1972 replacement.

Ross-on-Wye

The tall spire of St Mary's is a very prominent landmark in the Ross-on-Wye area, reflecting the dimensions of this large parish church. Built of rich red sandstone in the 13th century, the church has interesting stonework and other features. The east window shows four complete 15th-century figures, and the Markye Chapel is notable for two large Perpendicular arches supported on an octagonal pier. In the churchyard are the elm trees planted by John Kyrle, 'the man of Ross' who created the Prospect Gardens and did other good work for the town.

Rowlstone

On high ground overlooking the Golden Valley, the church of St Peter at Rowlstone is noted for its fine decoration – outstanding examples of the Herefordshire School of Romanesque Sculpture.

St Margaret's

Located high in the hills at the western end of the Golden Valley, this simple medieval church features an intricately-carved Welsh-style rood screen.

Shobdon

Built in the Gothic style in 1756 on the site of an earlier church, this is the only Roccoco church in England. It is decorated in ornate painted plasterwork with motifs of Chinese origin, and all the furniture and fittings are in the same style. Surviving from the earlier church, and standing in surrounding parkland, are fine examples of Romanesque arches, equal in the quality of their craftsmanship to those at Kilpeck.

Walford

Dedicated to St Michael and All Angels, the church is of Norman origin. The north-east tower was once detached, and interior decoration includes Early English carvings. The east end has Perpendicular Gothic windows and was rebuilt in about 1430. Other notable features include the 15th-century font and the Cromwellian funeral helm.

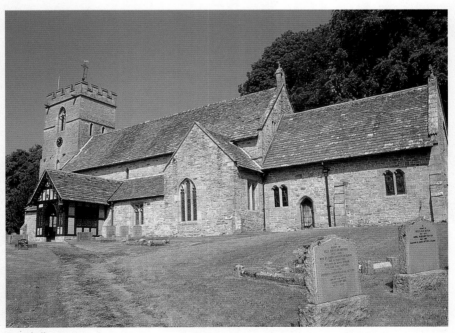

Lyonshall

Eadisley

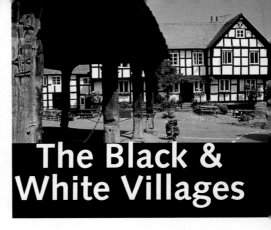

The Black & White Villages

Some of the most attractive and unspoilt villages in England are to be found in north-west Herefordshire – an area famous for its old black and white timber-framed buildings. This very distinctive architectural style is much in evidence in villages such as Eardisland, Pembridge, Eardisley and Weobley, as well as in the market towns of Leominster and Kington. A remarkable aspect of this timber-frame method of construction was that no nails were used – it was all done with pegs!

The churches too are reminders of the area's long history, containing records of people and events going back to the time of the Domesday Book and before. Today, these villages still retain a strong feeling of community, as a visit to any of the places described in the following will demonstrate.

Black & White Village Trail

This circular route of about 40 miles makes for an excellent day out. If you start at Leominster and travel in a clockwise direction on the A44, the trail takes you in turn to Dilwyn, Weobley, Sarnesfield, Kinnersley, Eardisley, Kington, Lyonshall, Pembridge and Eardisland.

Dilwyn

What could be more idyllic than an English village green sporting a spreading chestnut tree and overlooked by old timbered black and white cottages? Such is the charm of Dilwyn – a picture-postcard village which can easily convince you that you've stepped backwards into a time warp. For good measure, the pub is timber-framed too. The village church, dedicated to St Mary, has a medieval screen and a knight's tomb from the late 13th or early 14th century.

Eardisland

Many would argue that this village on the banks of the placid River Arrow is the prettiest in Herefordshire – a view echoed by a television poll in the Midlands' region.

There is certainly a great deal here to substantiate the claim. Eardisland, approximately five miles west of Leominster, has an astonishing abundance of timbered black and white buildings, all but a few of them fine examples of Herefordshire's traditional timber-and-plaster architecture. Many date from the 17th century and some are much older still. Along with these centuries-old houses and cottages are two village inns, a bowling green, dovecotes, and a church which is mostly early 13th century. Every year, between Easter and late autumn, it presents a major photographic exhibition depicting the county's churches.

One of the oldest treasures in Eardisland is Staick House, a timber-framed mansion dating from the 14th century. Built as a yeoman's hall, it retains many of the original windows and doors but it is privately owned and not open to visitors. Another fine historic house, Burton Court, stands a mile from the village and is a popular visitor attraction in its own right.

Like so many other English villages, Eardisland developed round a Norman castle. This one was built to guard a road between England and Wales – the same road taken by Henry Tudor in 1485 on his way to Bosworth Field to defeat Richard III and become Henry VII. No structural remains of the castle have survived, but the great moated mound where the keep once stood can still be seen.

Eardisley

Five miles south of Kington, Eardisley is a fascinating village whose associations with timber extend beyond its attractive black and white cottages and timber-frame architecture. At the time of Domesday, which describes the village as a clearing in the wood, Eardisley was in the centre of a vast forest, of which the only surviving tree is believed to be the oak now standing behind the old chapel on Hurstway Common close to the village. Known as the Great Oak of Eardisley, the tree has a thirty-foot circumference and an estimated age of between eight and nine hundred years.

Black and white half-timbered cottages line Eardisley's single street. Among the other timber-framed buildings of interest are the small 17th-century building now occupied by the village post office and a fine example of a 14th-century cruck building close to the village hall. This features massive curved timbers (cruck frames) enclosing three bays, one of which includes an inglenook fireplace.

The pump house supplied water to the village right up until the 1960's, when Eardisley was connected to the mains. The pump stands outside another cruck-framed building – one of the few to have remained in domestic use throughout its existence.

The most outstanding feature of the 12th-century village church of St Mary Magdalene is the Norman font of 1150. The work of the Herefordshire School of Romanesque sculpture, it is in remarkably fine condition and its ornamentation portrays a mix of Celtic, Saxon and Norman myths and beliefs. The village also had a Norman castle, destroyed in 1645 during the Civil War.

Tram Square marks the original market area in Eardisley and was once the venue for hiring fairs, where shepherds, ploughmen, labourers and house servants

Pembridge

would offer their services to prospective employers and hope to be taken on before nightfall. The square, at the north end of the village, takes its name from a horsedrawn tramway which operated between Brecon and Eardisley from 1818 until 1856.

While in Eardisley a visit to The New Strand is well worthwhile. The second-hand bookshop here has over 25,000 titles on display and operates a search service for out-of-print books. There is also a coffee house and licensed bar, offering everything from snacks to traditional English cuisine.

Pembridge

Six miles east of Kington on the River Arrow, picturesque Pembridge proudly boasts dozens of listed buildings and many fine examples of the black and white timber-framed architecture so characteristic of this corner of Herefordshire.

Pembridge

employers – a tradition which continued here right up until the 1920's.

Every street in Pembridge has houses dating back to the 14th and 15th centuries, and there are half-timbered cottages and inns scattered round the triangular medieval marketplace. The open market hall dates from the early 1500's, its roof supported by eight oak pillars.

Opposite the hall stands the New Inn, which was founded in 1311 but rebuilt in the 17th century after fire destroyed the original building. Featuring fine black and white work and said to be haunted by two ghosts, the inn is reputedly the place where the treaty following the Battle of Mortimer Cross was signed.

Stone steps lead up from the marketplace to a knoll and the church of St Mary, which has a remarkable detached wooden bell tower. Cruciform in style, the spacious church is a 14th-century replacement for an earlier Norman church. The tower, containing five bells, was built in the early 13th century and rebuilt in 1668 using much of the original timber. It was thoroughly renovated again in 1987 – a project which won a prestigious award for the village. The holes in the door are believed to be from musket shot in the Civil War, indicating that the tower was used as a place of refuge in times of siege.

Almshouses, originally called hospitals, were built to help the poor and alleviate poverty. Two rows of almshouses were built in Pembridge in the 17th century, one of them provided by a former Bishop of Winchester who also owned sixteen brothels in Southwark!

Another exceptional building in the village is King's House, now home to the Visitor Centre. Named after Robert King, an affluent merchant, it is a very fine example of early 16th-century close-set timbering. As well as supporting the building the close-timbered oak displayed

A unique octagonal detached bell tower, 14th-century church, moated manor house, ancient market hall, cruck-framed houses, old forges, wheelwrights, almshouses, working pottery, cider mill – you'll find them all in Pembridge, and a great deal more besides. No visitor could be the least bit surprised that the village has featured in numerous film and TV productions, such claims to fame including *Unconditional Love* and *Little Lord Fauntleroy*.

In the 13th to early 16th centuries, Pembridge was a prosperous borough. A charter granted in 1240 permitted the holding of a weekly market as well as a cowslip fair in May and a woodcock fair in November. These also became hiring fairs, when men and women in search of jobs advertised their skills to prospective

the owner's considerable wealth, but this kind of construction used so much timber that it later became illegal. The house features ornate carvings and mouldings, and the jetties to the front and rear were further architectural symbols of status. More insight into the skills and techniques of the craftsmen of the day is provided by the exposed wattle and daub panels.

A three-arched bridge crosses the River Arrow to a pleasant picnic area, and just a mile from the village is Dunkertons Cider Mill at Luntley, where organic Herefordshire cider is made using traditional methods and old varieties of cider apples.

Pembridge is also the centre of the parish. A wide range of accommodation is available in the area, from self-catering, b&b and public houses to 14th-century farmhouses, a Jacobean court and an English country home. The Visitor Centre offers all the help and information you need and will point you in the right direction to discover the area's wide variety of attractions. These include everything from cheese-making and herb gardens to activities such as fishing, riding, flying, painting, walking and cycling.

Pembridge Visitor Centre

Housed in an important 16th-century timber-frame building which during its long history has also served as an inn, the Visitor Centre has everything you need to help you make the most of your time in this part of historic Herefordshire.

The Centre offers an interactive tourist information point, free leaflets on the area, local accommodation lists, local crafts and gifts, tea rooms, log fires in winter and lawned gardens in summer. A small permanent display of historic artefacts is augmented by periodic exhibitions based on traditional village trades and crafts. There are also prints and original work of local

Eardisland

artists, some of which can be found nowhere else in the county. And you can arrange your cycle hire here and take advantage of the routes (suitable for families) which start from Pembridge.

For further information on any aspect of Pembridge, ring the Visitor Centre (open seven days a week, 10.00-5.00) on 01544 388761.

Guided walks

Guided walks for clubs, societies, schools and special-interest groups are organised by the Pembridge Amenity Trust, a registered charity which manages the village bell tower, market hall, millennium meadow and a number of visitor facilities. Lasting from between 30 minutes and two hours, and tailored to your specific needs, the walks explore the outstanding medieval and Tudor architecture of Pembridge. A small charge is payable and refreshments are available by prior arrangement. For further information and booking ring 01544 388761 (fax 01544 388762).

Weobley

Pronounced Webley and located 10 miles north-west of Hereford, this is one of the finest examples of a black and white village to be seen anywhere in England.

Fanning out from the wide central street is an abundance of delightful timber-framed buildings – inns, shops and townhouses – some dating from the early 1300's. The best house of all is The Leys, a tall, eight-gabled timbered farmhouse on the outskirts of the village. Built in 1589, it is ribbed with enormous chimneys and features strikingly carved timbers and pargetted panels in the central gable.

The picturesque 14th-century Red Lion Inn is one of several attractive pubs. At its rear is a well-preserved cruck building (shaped like an upturned boat).

The church of St Peter and St Paul, at the lower end of the village, was built by the Norman family of de Lacy. The tower and its tall spire date from the 14th century, as does the traceried eight-sided font. The church displays excellent examples of 13th-century and 14th-century craftsmanship and interesting monuments. Among the latter is the striking white marble statue of Colonel John Birch, an officer in Cromwell's army who died in 1691.

Weobley also tells of a long and colourful history. Established in the 7th century and recorded in Domesday, the village has staked numerous modest claims to fame over the centuries. A Norman castle of some size and importance once protected the village, though only earthworks remain today. Charles I passed this way, reputedly staying at one of the village inns in 1645 after the Battle of Naseby. Prosperity came and went too, created by a once-thriving market and glove-making and ale-making industries. And in the 18th century, Weobley achieved notoriety and recognition in quick succession – the former as a centre for witchcraft and the latter thanks to Benjamin Tomkins, who lived in the village and is credited with originating the breed of the much-prized Hereford beef cattle. More of Weobley's fascinating history is told in the village's small but engaging museum.

A visit to Weobley can take in other historic sites within easy striking distance. Close to the village is Fenhampton, a Jacobean house, and in the churchyard at nearby Sarnesfield lies John Abel, the king's master builder and creator of many timber-framed buildings still surviving in the county. A further two miles west, between Sarnesfield and Eardisley, is Kinnersley Castle. The house was reconstructed in about 1588 by Robert Vaughan and contains many interesting Elizabethan and Jacobean features.

Eardisland

M any of Herefordshire's museums and heritage centres do not make an admission charge, but donations are always welcome as the income helps to maintain these vital links with the county's past. Some of the attractions described here are open all year round, others are seasonal, so it is always advisable to ring first before travelling.

Museums & Heritage Centres

Bromyard Heritage Centre

Tells the story of the town, particularly the importance of hop growing to the area, past and present.

Based on an 18th-century stable block, this is the venue for the very popular Year of the Hop exhibition. It is open daily from Easter to the end of September, and admission is free. For further information ring 01885 482038.

Burton Court, Eardisland

The 14th-century Great Hall of this historic house displays an extensive costume collection. Other attractions include a model fairground and railway. See also page 17. For further information ring 01544 388231.

Butchers' Row House, Ledbury

Standing in a timber-framed building that was moved from the town centre, this charming folk museum in Church Lane houses a collection of fascinating objects relating to local history. Admission is free and it is open daily from Easter to the end of September. For further information ring 01531 632040.

Churchill House Museum and Hatton Gallery, Hereford

In a superb location at the top of Aylestone Hill, the museum and gardens present the most spectacular views of Hereford and the Welsh borders from anywhere in the city. The museum displays costumes, furniture, clocks, dolls, decorative arts and everyday Victorian objects in room settings of the 18th and 19th centuries. Works of local artist Brian Hatton, who was killed in the First World War, are displayed in the Hatton Gallery. During 2000 a temporary exhibition, Look Back to the Future, is showing fashion and designs inspired by the past.

Admission to the museum and gallery is free and opening times are 2.00-5.00pm, Wednesday, Thursday, Friday and Sunday, from Easter to September. For further information ring 01432 260693.

Cider Museum & King Offa Distillery, Hereford

See page 15.

Hereford Museum & Art Gallery

Museum built 1874 and art gallery and library were added and opened in 1912.

In 1998, won a major award for providing for visitors with disabilities.

Lending and reference libraries .

Showing throughout 2000 is an exhibition entitled Herefordshire: A Sense of Place, which embraces the themes of landscape, farming, folklore, childhood, warfare and cooking to explore the county's unique character. There are many hands-on activities for children and interactive photographic displays of Herefordshire past and present.

During 2000 the art gallery shows include Herefordshire Art On View, the works of local artist John Horwill (1927-1997), summer exhibition, Herefordshire Art & Crafts Society's Annual Exhibition, Herefordshire Annual Photography Festival, and the Annual Exhibition of the Society of Wood Engravers.

Admission is free and it is open all year round from Tuesday to Saturday, plus Sundays and bank holiday Mondays from April to September (closed Good Friday). For further information ring 01432 260692.

Herefordshire Regimental Museum, Hereford

The museum is home to a collection of uniforms, colours, medals, equipment, documents, photographs and other items of military interest. For further information and opening times, ring the Territorial Army Centre in Hereford on 01432 359917.

Kington Museum

Local life is vividly portrayed through fascinating domestic, agricultural and wartime displays. Or it is crammed full of fascinating memorabilia of the town's social history. Admission is free and the museum is open every day from early April to the end of September. There is also a tea shop. For further information ring 01544 231486.

The Judge's Lodging, Presteigne

Open every day from March to October, this magnificent award-winning museum offers audio tours and displays judges' rooms, servants' quarters, cells and a courtroom, all set on three floors. For further information ring 01544 260650.

Ledbury Heritage Centre

Occupying a splendid Elizabethan timber-framed building – a former grammar school – the Heritage Centre tells the story of Ledbury's long and colourful history and gives insight into the lives of people associated with the town, including John Masefield and Elizabeth Barrett Browning. It is open daily from Easter to October (in winter by appointment only) and admission is free. For further information ring 01531 636147.

Leominster Folk Museum

Open from Easter to the end of September, the museum houses a wide range of exhibits, from prehistoric times to items of domestic, military, agricultural, industrial and social interest. An extensive collection of rural artefacts includes the Aymestrey Beaker Burial Skeleton and works by accomplished local artist John Scarlett-Davies. Admission is free. For further information ring 01568 615186.

Market House Heritage Centre, Ross-on-Wye

This historic building dates from 1650 and is the ideal setting in which to present the history and heritage of Ross-on-Wye and the Wye Valley. Admission is free and it is open 7 days a week from April to October and 6 days a week (closed Sunday) from November to March. For more information ring 01432 260673.

The Old House, Hereford

At the heart of historic Hereford, this is one of the county's most famous black and white houses. It was built in 1621 and is furnished throughout in the style of the 17th century, giving visitors a feel of what it must have been like to live in Cromwell's day. Admission is free and it is open all year round from Tuesday to Saturday, plus Sundays and bank holiday Mondays from April to September (closed Good Friday). For further information ring 01432 260694.

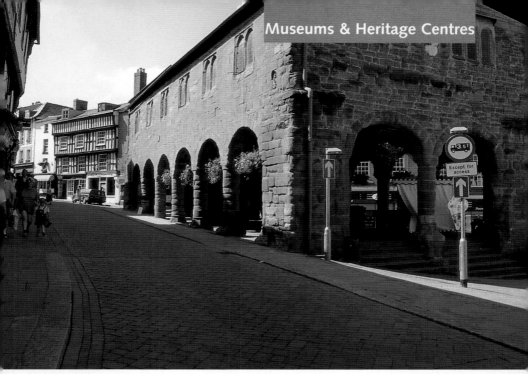

Ross-on-Wye

Railways in Miniature Museum, Ross-on-Wye

Models on display include British
locomotives from 1880-1947, Ross-on-Wye's
Great Western station, a mail coach and
other fascinating items. For further
information and opening times ring 01989
563394.

The Shambles, Newent, Gloucestershire

Not so much a museum, more a
complete Victorian village! Nestling within
the busy streets of the market town of
Newent is The Shambles – a remarkable
recreation of Victorian life, complete with
cobbled streets, alleyways, squares and a
fascinating variety of authentic buildings,
including a house, cottages, shops,
tradesmen's workshops, a mission chapel and
a Victorian conservatory. It all makes for a
very enjoyable day out, particularly as
Newent is an interesting town in its own

right and is close to other popular visitor attractions such as the Three Choirs Vineyard and the National Birds of Prey Centre. For further information about The Shambles, which opens from mid-March to December, ring 01531 822144.

St John Medieval Museum and Chapel, Hereford

The painstaking restoration of this 13th-century building illustrates how it was used as a hospital during the 17th century. Models of the Coningsby pensioners who used the hospital are on display in period dress and bandages, and a skeleton (thought to be that of a 15th-century abbot) remains in situ where it was discovered in the ruins. There is also an insight into the fascinating history of the Ancient Order of St John of Jerusalem and the wars it fought during the three hundred years of the Crusades. The museum is open five days a week (closed Monday and Friday) 2.00pm-5.00pm, from Easter to the end of September. For further information ring 01432 272837.

The Teddy Bear Museum, Bromyard

An Elizabethan setting in the town's old bakery in The Square is the treat for visitors to this museum of old bears, dolls and prams. It is open all year round. For further information ring 01885 488329.

Violette Szabo Museum, Wormelow

A new museum which is opening during 2000, it tells the story of the World War II heroine who was posthumously awarded the George Cross in 1946 after her execution by the Germans for her work with British Intelligence and the French Resistance. For further information ring 01981 540477.

The Waterworks Museum, Hereford

This time capsule of working machinery and social history tells the story of water supplies in Wales and the Marches over the last one hundred years. The variety of engines, pumps and equipment on display is unique, and some machines are the last examples of their kind working anywhere in the world. Moreover, the museum has no paid staff and takes great pride in maintaining all its engines in operating condition, thanks to the efforts of ex-engineers who give their time voluntarily.

The treasure of the collection is the oldest working triple-expansion steam engine in the UK. Standing two storeys high, its operation is awesome and it was capable of supplying Hereford with water from 1895 onwards. It was last used as a pump in 1953 and today is steamed purely to entertain visitors to the museum. Recent additions to the collection are a beam engine of 1851 and an Edwardian overshoot waterwheel.

Set in beautiful grounds close to the River Wye, the museum is accessible to visitors in wheelchairs and has a full range of facilities including children's activities. During summer there are fourteen in-steam open days. In addition, the Waterworks Museum welcomes group visits from Easter to October. For further information ring 01432 356653.

Weobley Museum

This small but fascinating village museum, housed in part of the old magistrate's court, puts the emphasis on the area's famous timber-framed buildings. Family history research material is also available. Admission is free. Opening times (April-September only) are limited so it is advisable to ring first on 01544 340292, or to check with a Tourist Information Centre.

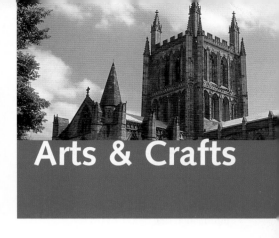

Arts & Crafts

Traditional arts and crafts have always played an important role in England's rural communities, and particularly in Herefordshire. Many of the skills that have been passed down from generation to generation over the centuries are still widely practiced today, as can be seen from the great variety of studios, workshops and galleries located across the county.

Visitors can also take advantage of a wide choice of arts and crafts holidays and courses – from painting and pottery for absolute beginners to antique print restoration, coracle making and contemporary dance. Details are available from any of Herefordshire's Tourist Information Centres.

Churchill House Museum and Hatton Gallery, Hereford
See page 43.

Collection Gallery, Ledbury
Selected for quality by the Crafts Council, this gallery represents artists whose work is rarely seen outside London. The collection includes jewellery, textiles, ceramics, wood and glassware. The gallery is open seven days a week and admission is free. For further information ring 01531 634641.

Hergest Court, Kington
This historic house, occupying a castle site dating back more than a thousand years, is now home to a gallery displaying an ever-changing collection of contemporary art. Fine art, ceramics, furniture and crafts are all to be found here. For further information ring 01544 231450.

Homend Pottery, Ledbury
This workshop, located on the main street in the town, produces hand-thrown and decorated creamware in distinctive designs. For further information ring 01531 634571.

Hop Pocket, Bishop's Frome
The work of more than 300 craftspeople, many local, is on display here. For further information ring 01531 640323.

Kemble Gallery, Hereford
Located in the city centre, near the cathedral, the gallery displays contemporary and traditional local crafts including ceramics, furniture, glass, rugs, wood, ironwork and other items. Opening hours are Monday to Saturday 9.30am-5.30pm and admission is free. For further information ring 01432 266049.

The Kilvert Gallery, Clyro, near Hay-on-Wye
The former home of the Victorian diarist, Francis Kilvert, is the setting for a constantly-changing exhibition of contemporary art and crafts. Many of the pieces, specially commissioned and designed, are by local artists and include fine art, furniture, ceramics and metalwork. There is an admission charge (redeemable on purchases over £10) and the gallery opens Tuesday to Sunday, plus bank holiday Mondays, 10.00am-5.00pm, Easter to the end of September (in winter by appointment only). For further information ring 01497 820831.

Lion Gallery, Leominster
Run as a non-profit-making venture, the gallery displays local arts and crafts. For further information ring 01568 611898.

The Lower Hundred, near Leominster

A small countryside workshop displaying local crafts and pottery. For further information ring 01584 711240.

Roger Oates Studio Shop, Eastnor

Leading British textile designers Roger Oates and Fay Morgan offer individual home accessories and gifts, including their highly distinctive rugs and runners. For further information ring 01531 631611.

Old Chapel Gallery, Pembridge

In the setting of a fine Victoria chapel, the gallery displays an ever-changing kaleidoscope of contemporary arts and crafts. Visitors will find an eclectic mix of work by both established local and nationally-known artists and makers and talented newcomers. Exhibitions are held seasonally four times a year and the gallery is open every day throughout the year. For further information ring or fax 01544 388842. Website: www.oldchapelgallery.co.uk

Michael Oxenham Studio & Gallery, Bromyard

Housed in a 16th-century building which was once the town's library, this studio is the base of professional countryside artist Michael Oxenham, whose work has appeared on numerous postage stamps. It is open for public viewing from Tuesday to Saturday. For further information ring 01885 482231.

Parkfields Gallery, Ross-on-Wye

Located within the grounds of a Georgian manor house, just a short journey from the town, Parkfields Gallery offers a warm and friendly welcome to all visitors. It is home to a whole spectrum of quality art forms by local and national artists, including painting, sculpture, ceramics, glassware and textiles that embrace the traditional and the avant-garde. Resident artists, who also welcome visitors, occupy three studios. Also available are refreshments, gifts and cards, and during 2000 the gallery's magnificent grounds will

host an outdoor sculpture exhibition entitled *Millennium Messages*. Parkfields Gallery is accessible to disabled visitors and opens daily, 10.00am-5.00pm (Sunday 12.00pm-4.00pm), with free admission and free parking. For further information ring 01989 750138.

Pembridge Terracotta

A very extensive choice of garden pots and tiles can be seen in this working pottery, set in a half-timbered barn. For further information ring 01544 388696.

Penrhos Gallery, Kington

The work of local artists and craftspeople is on display in the gallery. Exhibits include paintings, prints, photographs, textiles, woodwork, ceramics, glass, jewellery and sculptures in wood, metal and stone. For further information ring 01544 231555.

The Stable Studio, Kington

If you've always fancied yourself as an artist, or you want to improve your skill and technique, a two-day or three-day workshop at the Stable Studio will help you on your way. Over the last ten years the studio has become well established as a centre of first-class tuition, provided by artist Ronald Swanwick, one of the country's leading exponents of drawing and watercolour. The views from the studio's two-acre gardens provide plenty of subject matter and inspiration. For further information ring 01544 238871.

Wobage Farm Craft Workshops, Upton Bishop

Pottery, furniture and jewellery is produced here by a group of craftspeople. For further information ring 01989 780233 or 780495.

Wyebridge Interiors, Hereford

Sculptures in bronze or steel by internationally-renowned Walenty Pytel are available here, along with fabrics and interior design accessories. For further information ring 01432 350722.

Inside the Old Chapel Gallery

49

Hereford

Hereford has its origins in the Dark Ages and was once the Saxon capital of West Mercia. But it was the Romans who were hereabouts first, establishing their central settlement for the area at Kenchester, just five miles west of the present-day cathedral city. An impressive Roman mosaic, evidence of their occupation, now adorns the staircase in Hereford Museum, Art Gallery and Library.

After the Romans deserted Britain early in the 5th century in a vain attempt to protect what remained of their crumbling empire, the settlement at Kenchester was abandoned. The Saxons chose an alternative site, favouring a more strategic position on the north bank of the Wye, where the river could be forded at two points. The seeds for Hereford as we see it today had been sewn.

These were turbulent times. The land south of the Wye was then in Wales, and Welsh princes and chieftains not only fought each other for supremacy of their respective territories but also made frequent incursions across the border to take on the English. The Saxon King Offa walled in his new stronghold north of the river to keep them out, but for centuries Hereford, as it was to become, was constantly in the front line as successions of English and Welsh armies opposed each other.

Despite the conflict – or perhaps as a direct result of it – embryonic Hereford became a religious centre at a very early stage. It has been the seat of a bishop since at least 676 and was probably established as a cathedral centre by the end of the 7th century. The cathedral which lies at the heart of the city today is mainly Norman, dating back to 1080.

The Normans also built a castle in Hereford. In fact, to be precise, there have been two Norman castles here – the first, made of wood, built by the Norman nephew of Edward the Confessor and burned down by the Welsh in 1055, and the second, constructed with stone, replacing it shortly after the conquest of 1066. All that's left as a reminder that either castle ever existed is Castle Green, an open area by the river once enclosed by the bailey of the later castle. The duck pool formed part of its moat, and the motte was flattened in the 18th century to make way for redevelopment in the town.

Hereford

Hereford

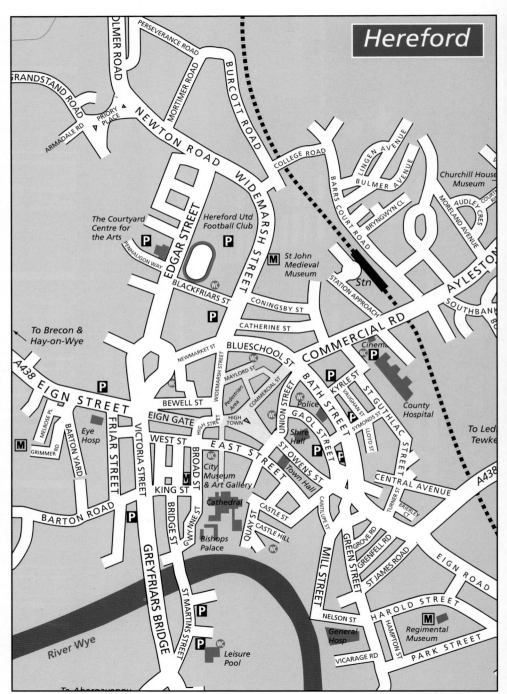

Hereford

The Green Dragon

Broad Street, Hereford HR4 9BG
Tel: (0)870 400 8113 Fax: (0)143 235 2139
email: HeritageHotels_Hereford.Green_Dragon@forte-hotels.com

The Green Dragon hostelry was already old when bishops sought planning permission for the city's magnificent cathedral, home of the medieval Mappa Mundi. Spick and span villages of black and white houses and churches look as though they were built yesterday. For those seeking intellectual sustenance there is Hay-on-Wye, the second hand book capital of the world and for the inner man, there are regular appearances on the Green Dragon's restaurant menu of such delights as Wye Valley salmon, Herefordshire hop cheese and Herefordshire beef.

Facilities

- 48 bedrooms *(2 four posters, 3 suites)*
- Restaurant • Bar • Lounge
- Free car park
- Baby listening/sitting

Directions

The Green Dragon sits right in the centre of Hereford, on Broad Street, north west of the Cathedral

Hereford grew at a slow pace under Norman rule, staying within the confines of its medieval walls. These were demolished in the 1770's. Cattle and sheep drovers passed through, bringing prosperity as a market town, and in the 18th century Hereford became something of fashionable winter resort much favoured by the county's gentry. Many of the substantial red-brick houses they built can still be seen. And by the end of the 19th century, following the arrival of the railways in the 1850's, Hereford had become established as an important regional administrative, social and industrial centre, a position it enjoys today.

One of the great charms of 21st-century Hereford is that despite its status as a city, it retains the distinctly unhurried pace of life more akin to those early days as a rural market town. The pedestrianised streets of the city centre, the public parks and gardens, the fascinating architectural mix, the natural attractions of the River Wye and the reassuring presence of the cathedral all add up to a pleasing and unique cocktail much appreciated by residents and visitors alike.

The south part of the town where it borders the Wye is particularly attractive. Here are the cathedral grounds, Castle Green and the Victoria Suspension Bridge, which is a pedestrian link built in 1898 after Queen Victoria's Diamond Jubilee to give access to the vast expanse of Bishop's Meadow and its riverside walks.

On a trip to Hereford you can enjoy first-class shopping, sample the best cider in the world, have a flutter on the racecourse, picnic by the river and discover two of Britain's most important historical treasures – the medieval Mappa Mundi and the Chained Library – in the great cathedral's newest building. Very few other cities offer so much variety in such compact, medieval streets, the layout of which has changed little since Saxon times. And very few other cities boast such an idyllic border location, surrounded on all sides by magnificent countryside.

BROOMY HILL, HEREFORD

The Waterworks Museum - Hereford is a hundred year time capsule of working machinery and social history which tells the story of water supplies in Wales and the Marches. The range of engines, pumps and equipment on display is unique. Some machines are the last examples of their kind working anywhere in the world.

The treasure of this collection is the oldest working triple expansion steam engine in the UK. It stands two floors high and is quite awesome in operation. This engine was capable of supplying Hereford with water from 1895 onwards, being last used to pump water for real in 1953. Now it is steamed purely for the pleasure of visitors. Recent additions to the collection are a beam engine of 1851 and an Edwardian overshot waterwheel.

The museum prides itself on having all its engines in operating condition. The staff are mainly ex-engineers and give their time and energy voluntarily. The Museum has no paid staff.

Set in lovely grounds close to the river Wye on the outskirts of Hereford, this friendly Museum is accessible by those in wheelchairs and has a full range of visitor facilities. There is an abundance of social history as well as the magnificent working engines. A series of wall displays tells the history of water supplies in the area over 2000 years. Children's activities are provided and there are booklets about the Museum for all ages from pre-school to teens.

The Waterworks Museum has fourteen public open days in steam each summer season but in addition welcomes Group visits from Easter to October. There is always a warm welcome.

In steam days open 2-5pm:
Easter, Spring & August Bank
Holiday Sunday/Monday
Last Sunday in month
April-September
Second Sunday in month
June-September
Also open every Tuesday 11-4
from Easter to September,
not in steam.
Information 01432 356653
Registered Charity -
Registered Museum

all.bar.one

This restaurant and cafe bar, which opened in February 2000, is described as Hereford's newest and most innovative eating place. It is located in West Street and opens Monday to Saturday from 11.00am-11.00pm. For further information and bookings ring 01432 265950.

The Barrels & Wye Vallery Brewery

The Barrels is an 18th-century pub in St Owen Street which brews its own traditional ales at the rear of the premises. Wye Valley Brewery is the oldest brewery in Hereford. For further information ring 01432 342546.

Breakaway Survival School

If the idea of getting back to nature appeals to you, maybe you'd like to put yourself in the hands of an ex-member of the SAS for a weekend you'll never forget. Then again, maybe you wouldn't! On a Breakaway Survival course you'll spend a couple of cold nights in the Brecon Beacons with little more than a plastic sheet for a bed and instruction on skills such as catching and cooking rabbits, building a shelter and how to avoid getting lost. To find out more – if you dare – you'll have to ring 01432 267097.

Bulmers Cider Mill

See page 15.

Cathedral Cruises

A 40-minute cruise with commentary is the most relaxing way to explore the river and enjoy unique views of this historic cathedral city. For further information ring 01432 358957.

Churchill House Museum

See page 43.

Cider Museum & King Offa Distillery

See page 15.

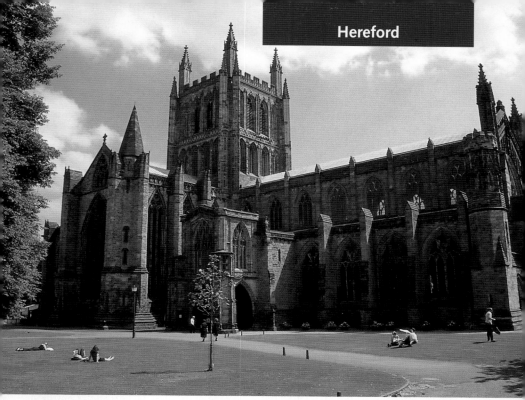

Hereford Cathedral

The Courtyard Centre for the Arts

This stunning new building, built in 1998, has a three-storey glass facade and presents a varied programme of entertainment embracing theatre, dance, music, comedy and film. It also incorporates an art gallery, cafe, bar and restaurant. For further information ring 01432 359252.

Hagley Court Vineyard

A family-run vineyard and garden with superb views. For further information ring 01432 850003.

Hereford Cathedral

A masterpiece in sandstone, Hereford Cathedral is richly endowed with all manner of priceless treasures. The present building was consecrated in the 1140's and has been greatly restored, its architecture inspiring a painting by Turner.

The cathedral's Norman origins and workmanship are most evident in the massive pillars (each seven feet in diameter) and arches of the 12th-century nave and the arches supporting the central tower. The tower, completed in 1315, now has a 20th-century corona suspended beneath it. The north and south aisles are also 14th century.

There are many other features of interest. They include the Norman font (c1150), the fine Early English Lady Chapel (1220), the Tudor Audley Chantry of 1500, the Bishop Stanbury Chantry Chapel (1496), tapestries by John Piper, a mosaic and statue of St Ethelbert, memorial brasses, the Shrine of St Thomas of Hereford, The Becket Reliquary – one of the few remaining caskets in existence made for the specific purpose of holding a relic of Canterbury's St Thomas – and of course the Mappa Mundi and Chained Library Exhibition.

There are also a number of useful and interesting visitor services: Information Desk, Cathedral Shop, Brass Rubbing Centre and The Cathedral Restaurant. For any further information ring 01432 374200.

Hereford Leisure Centre
Adjacent to Hereford Racecourse, the centre has facilities for a wide variety of indoor sports, as well as a sauna and fitness suite, and the racecourse itself accommodates a nine-hole golf course and a floodlit athletics track.

Hereford Museum & Art Gallery
See page 43.

Hereford Racecourse
For race fixtures and other information, ring 01432 273560.

Jungle Mania Adventure Playground
Open 7 days a week, this all-weather soft indoor playground offers 6,000 square feet of fun and adventure for kids up to 12 years old. There is a special area for the under-5's and a lounge area for parents. For further information ring 01432 263300.

Kemble Gallery
See page 47.

Kenchester Water Gardens
See page 25.

Leisure Pool
Facilities include main leisure pool, learner pool, fitness suite, sauna, sun bed and cafe. Tennis is available on nearby Bishop's Meadow.

Mappa Mundi and Chained Library Exhibition, Hereford Cathedral
Here are two of Britain's most important historical treasures, housed in Hereford Cathedral's magnificent new library, which

City Centre of Hereford

was generously funded by John Paul Getty Junior and in 1997 won the Royal Fine Art Commission's Building of the Year Award.

The medieval Mappa Mundi (Map of the World) was drawn on vellum in the late 13th century by Richard de Bello, a prebendary of the cathedral. It is a circular map depicting his interpretation of the known world at that time, with Jerusalem at the centre surrounded by Asia, Africa and Europe. Its decoration includes biblical stories, mythical beasts and other fanciful designs. It is regarded as the most remarkable 13th-century illustrated English manuscript.

The Chained Library is the finest in Britain and the largest in the world. It contains 1500 rare books, including over 200 medieval manuscripts, chained to their original 17th-century book presses. The library was founded in Saxon times , when the Ango-Saxon gospels, written in about 800, were given to the cathedral.

Hereford Cathedral from the River Wye

Entrance to the new building is via the interpretative exhibition, housed in the cathedral's 15th-century south-west cloister, which tells the story of these great national treasures through models, original artefacts and the latest interactive computer technology. In fact, both the exhibition and the building themselves have been described as works of art.

For further information ring Hereford Cathedral on 01432 374200.

Moccas Court
See page 21.

The Old House
See page 44.

Overcroft Garden Nursery
See page 26.

St John Medieval Museum & Chapel
See page 46.

TGS Bowling
If you want the guarantee of first-class tenpin bowling and great fun, this is the place to head for. Twelve computerised lanes, air conditioning, a pro shop, pool, the latest video games and amusements, American bar and bistro, Sunday lunches, and the outrageous new Xtreme bowling system which enables you to play in the dark! What's more, TGS Bowling, located in Station Approach, is open every day of the week from 10.00am till late, with free admission and ample free parking. For further information ring 01432 352500.

TASTE FOR
Adventure
CENTRE

Registered Charity No. 1027330

Situated on the outskirts of this Historic Town and within close proximity to some of Herefordshires idyllic Black and White villages is The Taste for Adventure Centre. Founded in 1991 by ex SAS sergeant major and Everest summiteer (1976) 'Brummie' Stokes BEM MISM to help less privileged children and take them out into the great outdoors climbing, abseiling, caving, mountain biking etc.

We cater for large groups of people at any one time, the centre itself is clean, bright and homely, comprising of a large living dining room, bunk bed accommodation sleeping up to 18 people and shower rooms. All safety equipment and public liability insurance is provided in the price and all of our instructors hold governing body awards for all the activities we provide.

If it is not an activity holiday you are looking for and you just want a base so you can go off and do some sight seeing in the area, then the centre also has its own self catering, two bedroom annex which is purpose built for the disabled, it can sleep up to seven people and of course is suitable for a family holiday where you can take part in some of the activities on offer.

We also run various courses for the corporate market, which include leadership, communication, planning, ideas, and team building problem solving courses.
Taste for adventure is growing all the time, this year we are building a new office, lecture/conference room and a state of the art climbing tower/high level ropes course, to test and challenge everyone, this will prove to be an exhilarating experience for all.
What we offer is good safe fun for everyone from the age of 10 years upwards, for more information or to come for a visit you can contact us on 01432 761398. We are a non profit making charity, therefore when you book with us you are helping the children that we help.

- **State of the Art Climbing Tower**
- **High Level Ropes Course**
- **Climbing/Abseiling • Caving**
- **Kayaking/Canoeing • Mountain Biking**
- **Archery • Zip Wire • Assault Course**

The Hafod, Credenhill, Hereford, HR4 7DA
Tel & Fax: 01432 761398
email: tfac@credenhill99.freeserve.co.uk
website: www.credenhill99.freeserve.co.uk

Waterworks Museum
See page 46.

Weastern Adventure
Groups of all ages can enjoy exciting outdoor activities such as climbing, abseiling, canoeing, caving, gorge walking and mountain walking. For further information ring 01432 279030.

Weir Garden
See page 27.

Wyebridge Interiors
See page 49.

Cruising the River Wye

A-Z of Herefordshire

The following is a quick-reference guide to the county's towns, villages and hamlets and the attractions they hold for visitors.

Abbey Dore

In this quiet village at the southern end of the River Dore's Golden Valley stand the original tall choir and transepts of a Cistercian monastery church whose nave has long since disappeared. The church, built after 1180, was too big for the little village of Abbey Dore and was actually constructed to serve a large monastic community. After the dissolution of the monastery under Henry VIII, and a subsequent century of decay, the remains were restored at length in the 1630's by Lord Scudamore, and the transept murals, screen, ceiling, tower and east window glass showing the Ascension all date from this time. The fine Norman interior is enormous.

Across the River Dore from the church is Abbey Dore Court. This grand old house has an impressive walled garden which is open to visitors.

Almeley

The timbered 17th-century meeting house is one of the oldest in England, and the church has a 16th-century roof.

Bacton

A tiny village in the Golden Valley, where the church houses a monument showing Elizabeth I and one of her maids of honour – possibly a local girl who might have made the exquisite 400-year-old altar cloth.

Ballingham

The church of St Dyfrig stands apart from the village, close to 17th-century Ballingham Hall. St Dyfrig (also known as St Dubricius) was a 6th-century Welsh prince who established religious communities and colleges in several places between the Wye and the Black Mountains. He became the first bishop of Llandaff and died on Bardsey Island (the burial place of saints) off the coast of north-west Wales.

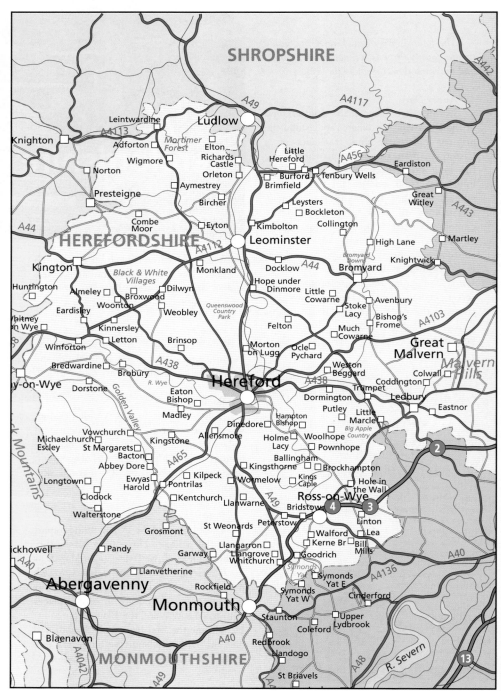

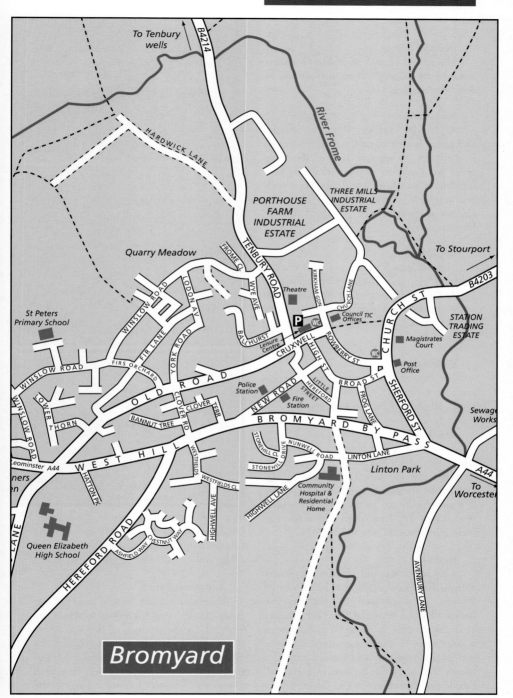

Bromyard

Bishop's Frome

The rebuilt church of St Mary's retains some of its original Norman features, as described on page 31.

Blakemere

A hamlet rather than a village, Blakemere is centred on the small church of St Leonard. Along one side of the wide green are a number of impressive Georgian farmhouse and farm buildings, built with characteristic warm red brick. Near the church are several well-preserved timber-framed cottages.

Bockleton

This village's Norman and later church contains the fine Barnley monument of 1594. Old mounting steps approach the 15th-century lych-gate, and Bockleton Court Farm displays a number of interesting Jacobean features.

Bodenham

The church, 13th century in part, has a massive tower. Broadfield Court, to the north, originates from the 14th century.

Brockington Golf Club

Bodenham is also home to Brockington Golf Club, which has an undulating course (par 66 for 18 holes) of 4,688 yards. Divided by a winding brook and two ponds, it a real challenge to most golfers and is open every day from dawn till dusk. For further information ring 01568 797877.

Bosbury

This attractive and traditional village, with its wide main street and half-timbered houses, is dominated by the massive detached stone tower of the 12th-century Holy Trinity church. Believed to have been a large town in pre-Saxon times, Bosbury was once prosperous and formed part of a manor owned by the bishops of Hereford. Beside the churchyard is Old Court, at one

time the country residence of the bishops. Other buildings of interest include the Elizabethan free grammar school and the village inn.

Brampton Bryan

Brampton Bryan has a large village green, around which pleasant cottages are grouped. In the grounds of the hall where the Harley family lived are the remains of a 14th-century castle – the site of a famous siege in the Civil War, in which Brampton Bryan was stoutly defended against the

Bromyard

Royalist forces by Lady Brilliana Harley in the absence of her husband. She died a few weeks later. The siege saw the destruction of the church, which was rebuilt in 1656 and has an interesting hammer-beam roof.

Bredwardine

Standing on the River Wye, Bredwardine is the burial place of diarist Francis Kilvert, who came here as vicar in 1877 and died two years later at the age of only 38. The church where he preached is remarkable in its own right. The building stands askew, the walls bulging very markedly to the south, and a sandstone slab lintel over the north doorway is carved with two strange figures. Many of the houses in the village from Kilvert's time still survive, including the vicarage where he lived, the Red Lion Hotel (an excellent base for walkers and anglers) and 14th-century Old Court. The elegant six-arch bridge spanning the river is another notable feature – one of the finest old bridges to be found on the Wye.

The Moccas Fishery: Run by the owners of the Red Lion Hotel in Bredwardine, the fishery offers 7 miles of the River Wye and a small carp lake. Salmon, trout, barbel, chub and pike are the main species of the Wye, with wild carp, tench and rudd in the lake. Twenty-peg match fishing is also available, as is comfortable hotel accommodation. For further information ring 01981 500303.

Brockhampton

The village is notable for its interesting church, as described on page 32.

Bromyard

Situated midway between the two cathedral cities of Hereford and Worcester (a distance of 15 miles and 14 miles respectively), Bromyard is a thriving community which also supports a significant rural population in surrounding villages and hamlets. The pleasant town centre is bypassed by the busy A44 and makes for leisurely shopping and browsing in the High Street and small Hop Market square. There's also an interesting mixture of architectural styles, including some outstanding timber-framed buildings such as an inn and a well-restored three-storey building, now an art gallery. Church Street leads from The Square to St Peter's church, which is mainly 14th-century but with surviving Norman work and an unusual castellated exterior stair turret to the tower.

Between the River Frome and the town is the site of the old railway station, which was opened in May 1877 by the Worcester and Bromyard Railway Company. The line was sold to the Great Western Railway in 1888, and in 1897 a further single-track line between Bromyard and Leominster was put into service. By 1900 five trains a day were running from Worcester to Leominster via Bromyard. The line between Bromyard and Worcester survived for 87 years before closing in 1964.

Rising steeply to the east of the the town is Bromyard Downs, a popular local beauty spot. It is a high, wide and open area of grass and bracken, topped by Warren Wood, and the views towards Wales and the Midlands are stunning.

Bromyard Heritage Centre
See page 43.

Bromyard Leisure Centre
Located in Cruxwell Street, it offers many indoor sports including badminton, short-mat bowling and five-a-side soccer. Also available are a multi-gym, sauna, sunbed and fully licensed bar. For further information ring 01885 482195.

Lower Brockhampton
See page 21.

Michael Oxenham Studio & Gallery
See page 48.

St Peter's Church
See page 32.

The Teddy Bear Museum
See page 46.

The Conquest Theatre
The theatre presents a regular and varied programme throughout the year.

Leominster Market

CANOE & KAYAK HIRE @ SYMONDS YAT EAST

The Symonds Yat Gorge provides Wyedean Canoe & Adventure Centre with the best location in the country for the novice or expert canoeist. Our exclusive facilities on the banks of the Wye comprise 30 Canadian open canoes, 30 single kayaks and all necessary peripheral equipment.

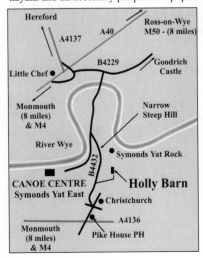

The safe, clean waters of the Wye provide the ideal environment for the complete beginner to develop basic canoe strokes, balance and canoe control, all supervised by our qualified instructors.

Set in some of the most beautiful countryside in the whole of Great Britain, Wyedean Canoe & Adventure Centre is easily accessible by major road links - the M50/A40 brings you down from the Midlands and for those arriving from the South, once over the Severn Bridge, from the M4/M5 junction, you can either head for the A40 at Monmouth,via the Wye Valley, or through the Forest of Dean to Coleford, and then out to the Centre at Symonds Yat Rock

Freephone: 0800 3281235
To book or request our new brochure.
Canoe Centre: 01600 890129
Mobile: 0421 472817

Castle Frome

The church here has a remarkable Norman font with grotesque carvings.

Clodock

St Clodock, a British saint, was the grandson of King Brychan of Brecknockshire. Sixty churches are dedicated to various members of his family. The village stands on the River Monnow and the church contains a Norman chancel with a three-decker pulpit and a west gallery.

Coleford

Standing south of Symonds Yat East in the Forest of Dean, Coleford is a town whose roots lie in the industry born from the forest's coal and iron ore deposits. It was the home of the Mushet family, pioneers in the manufacture of cast steel. The town is also notable for its fine large Victorian chapels, built for the workers whose hands forged the industry, and remains of the enormous blast furnaces that smelted the iron ore can still be seen.

Colwall

This big, sprawling village lies on the wooded western slopes of the Malvern Hills, and in the centre stands Colwall Stone – a large piece of limestone which is the subject of much local legend. The Herefordshire Beacon (see page 9) is reached from the top of the village.

Cradley

Historic buildings are clustered around the church, which is largely Victorian. These include the 15th-century timber-framed school, the Georgian rectory and other attractive timber-framed houses. The village also has a modern shopping area.

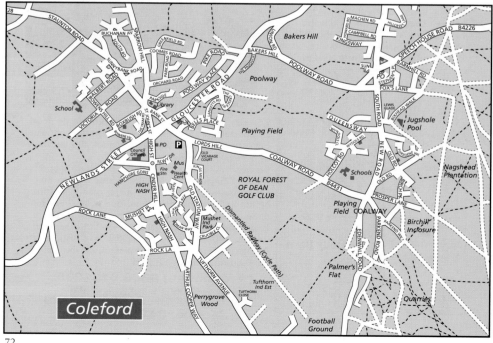

Coleford

Craswall

The Bull's Head at Craswall is one of the loneliest pubs in the district and one of the least affected by the outside world, serving a scattered village community of only 200 people. It merits a visit in its own right as one of the few pubs of its kind still in existence. Behind the plain and lonely little church of St Mary's is a grassy hollow where cockfights once took place. To the north, the ruins of Craswall Priory lie hidden among trees in a deep valley.

Dorstone

Lying near the head of the Golden Valley, about 6 miles east of Hay-on-Wye, the village has a rebuilt church which retains a 13th-century tower arch. The church was reputedly founded by John de Brito to atone for his part in the murder of Thomas a Becket in 1171. Close to the village are Arthur's Stone – the remains of a late Neolithic long barrow – and the ruins of medieval Snodhill Castle. In medieval times, markets were held in Dorstone.

Vowchurch

Eardisland

See page 37.

Eardisley

See page 38.

Eastnor

Eastnor boasts two castles – Bronsil Castle, a 15th-century ruin destroyed in the Civil War, and the other the stunning 19th-century Eastnor Castle, built to the design of Sir Robert Smirke, who also designed the British Museum. The latter is finely furnished and stands in a beautiful park, as described on page 18. The delightful estate village of Eastnor is grouped around the entrance to Eastnor Castle. The picturesque cottages, post office, school and rectory all date from the 19th century, and there is a well on the green. Footpaths from the village take you up to an obelisk on the Malverns, from where there are superb views across the castle, grounds and lake.

Eyton

The village stands on the River Lugg and is notable for two buildings – Eyton Court, which has a black and white wing from the 16th century, and the church, an interesting feature of which is a beautiful 15th-century rood screen and loft.

Fownhope

Standing on the banks of the Wye, Fownhope has one of the largest churches in Herefordshire, notable for its Norman tower (see page 32). There is also an Elizabethan timbered mansion called the Court. Close to the village are the sites of two prehistoric camps.

Garway

In the rebuilt church at Garway, a small village in beautiful unspoilt countryside on the River Monnow, there is a fine example of Norman craftsmanship in the chancel.

Hay-on-Wye

The huge semi-detached tower is also of interest. Nearby is a circular 14th-century dovecote which once belonged to the Knights Templars.

Goodrich

This small village near Ross-on-Wye is famous for the ruins of its mighty 12th-century castle, which like so many others was destroyed by Cromwell during the Civil War. The castle's elevated position above the River Wye makes it a popular visitor attraction, as described on page 19.

The village itself lies in a hollow between the castle and the church. The houses are built of pale sandstone and greystone, and their Gothic flavour is best exemplified by Ye Hostelrie Hotel (described below), which dates from 1830.

Ye Hostelrie Hotel: Another distinctive building in Goodrich is this hospitable family-run hotel, whose pinnacles and tall latticed windows dominate the small main street. All bedrooms are en suite and individually decorated, and there are two elegant restaurants, a bar, an attractive garden and patio, and ample parking. For further information and bookings ring 01600 890241.

Great Malvern

Great Malvern, a picturesque and popular spa town which in the past enjoyed great prosperity, is the largest of several towns in the area which cluster on the slopes of the Malvern Hills beneath the towering height of the Worcestershire Beacon (1,395 feet). About 40 square miles of the hills are designated an Area of Outstanding Natural Beauty, and it is no enigma that Elgar found such inspiration here for his music. His burial place is four miles to the south at Little Malvern.

In the town of Great Malvern, which lies on the Worcestershire side of the ridge that forms a natural divide between this county and Herefordshire, is Malvern Priory

– a fine Norman and perpendicular church of cathedral-like splendour, containing a great deal of old glass and examples of remarkable encaustic tiles. Malvern College is a well-known school, and local drama festivals are famous for the performances of plays by George Bernard Shaw. Below the town is the vast Three Counties Showground, the venue for major events throughout the year. Another attraction in this classic English spa town is the beautifully-renovated railway station – a nostalgic reminder of how country railways used to be in the glorious steamy days of the Great Western.

Hay-on-Wye

A true border town, with one foot in England and the other in Wales, Hay-on-Wye is situated at the north-east corner of the Brecon Beacons National Park amidst the beautiful countryside of the Wye Valley. In the south it is overlooked by the Black Mountains, from which Hay Bluff rises to 2,219 feet.

At one time divided into Welsh Hay and English Hay, the town now enjoys international fame and prosperity as the world's largest centre for secondhand books – an achievement due to Richard Booth, whose business is based in Hay Castle. First-time visitors are frequently overwhelmed that such a small and attractive market town can house so many books, which are for sale on every subject, every corner and in virtually every shop. Not surprisingly, the annual Hay-on-Wye festival has become a major literary event that attracts visitors and guest writers from all corners of the world.

The market has been held in the town since 1233, but it was in about 1150 that the Marcher Lord Roger, Earl of Hereford, built a castle and established a walled town here. The Norman gateway and tower of the present castle are the remains of a stronghold built subsequently. The 13th century was a bad time for Hay, when border upheavals saw it burned, destroyed and besieged in turn by King John, Llewelyn the Great and the forces of Edward I. In about 1400 it was also attacked by Owain Glyndwr, who destroyed the castle.

Diarist Francis Kilvert was a frequent visitor to Hay Castle, which at that time was the residence of the vicar of Hay. The parish church of St Mary dates mainly from 1834, when it was rebuilt and enlarged, but it still retains features dating from the 13th century.

In summer, Hay is alive with the bustle and excitement of literary and jazz festivals, and in December the streets take on a Dickensian atmosphere with brightly-lit shop windows, street entertainers, stalls, and the aroma of roasting chestnuts and potatoes.

Paddles & Pedals

The river and magnificent countryside make Hay-on-Wye an excellent base for a variety of sporting and leisure activities. Paddles & Pedals, in Castle Street, specialises in canoe and kayak hire on a half-day and full-day basis, with free return transport, and also sells and repairs bikes at competitive rates. For further information ring 01497 820604.

Hereford

See page 50.

Hoarwithy

The pretty village of Hoarwithy, on the Wye, is remarkable for its Italianate church – the dream of William Poole, vicar here from 1854 for more than fifty years, who dug deep into the family coffers to transform a dilapidated chapel into a fantasy that is in astonishing contrast to the

Hoarwithy

Norman and medieval churches so characteristic of Herefordshire. The church's tall campanile dominates the village, and features include a cloister walk, four massive Byzantine capped pillars, mosaic flooring, romanesque windows and lots of stained glass. In the village is a charming inn and a bridge with a Gothic toll house – a good starting point for riverside walks and views.

Holme Lacy

The church stands in meadows outside the village. It is full of elaborate marble monuments to the Scudamore family, who gained the estate through marriage to the Lucy Marcher Lords.

Hope-under-Dinmore

The village's restored church has a sculptured 13th-century font and fine Coningsby monuments. A mile to the south

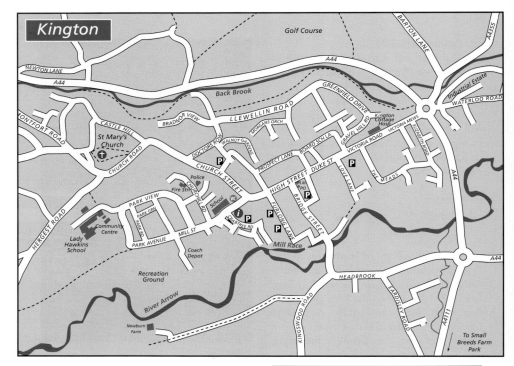

of the village is Dinmoor Hill – a viewpoint overlooking the Lugg Valley. Nearby are several buildings of historic interest – 16th-century Dinmore Manor, the Hospitallers' Church (12th-14th century) and Hampton Court (a fine castellated house of 15th-century origin but greatly restored, the gardens of which are now open to visitors as described on page 27).

Kilpeck

The village's beautiful little Norman church of St Mary and St David – the jewel in the crown of all Herefordshire's churches and one of the most remarkable little churches in Britain – is rich with rare sandstone carving, reminiscent of Celtic craftsmanship and representing the pinnacle of the Herefordshire School of Sculpture. For further information see page 33.

River Wye

King's Caple

The village of King's Caple stands among cider apple orchards. The church is set on a knoll and enjoys superb views over the rolling countryside. It was built with a nave wide enough to accommodate King John and his companions on their hunting trips to the Royal Forest here.

Kingsland

The Battle of Mortimer Cross was fought just half a mile from the village. The 13th-century church contains the curious Volca chamber.

Kingston

This is the only town in Herefordshire to stand on the western side of Offa's Dyke, on the Welsh-English border – but Kington has been part of England for a thousand years. Significant for its agriculture and its strategic position, this small market town grew in importance during the Industrial Revolution and established a horsedrawn tramway to link it with the coalmines and steelworks of South Wales. Local industry also developed, aided by watermills on the River Arrow and the Back Brook.

Today, like Bromyard, Kington benefits enormously from having been bypassed by the A44. The atmosphere is very much that of a border town – part English, part Welsh. At the western end of the High Street is the tall clock tower, from which Castle Street leads up to St Mary's church. Overlooking the town from its hilltop location, it was built around 1200 but greatly restored and enlarged in the Victorian era. The stained glass is 19th-century but in late medieval style. Outside, the mound is all that remains of the castle. Other buildings of interest in Kington include the old grammar school of 1625, designed by John Abel, the market hall of 1885 and 1897, and the former town hall of 1845.

Kington is north Herefordshire's gateway to mid-Wales and is surrounded by beautiful countryside. Above the town on Bradnor Hill is England's highest golf course. On the town's outskirts are two of the county's top attractions – Hergest Croft Gardens and The Small Breeds Farm Park and Owl Centre.

Offa's Dyke is not the only long-distance footpath to pass through the town: the Mortimer Trail cuts a 30-mile route along a succession of ridges between Kington and Ludlow. For visitors with the energy to explore the borderlands there is much to see, such as the Elan Valley and the historic Welsh towns of New Radnor and Presteigne.

Kington Museum
See page 44.

River Wye

Kington Leisure Centre

Offering a range of sporting and recreational activities, the leisure centre is located within Lady Hawkins School. For more information ring 01544 230488.

Offa's Bikes

Cycling is a very rewarding way in which to explore this fascinating and beautiful border area, and bike hire is available here at competitive rates. For more information ring 01544 230534.

Kington Golf Club

The highest course in England and Wales, with superb views over the Black Mountains and Offa's Dyke. For further information ring 01544 230340.

Hergest Croft Gardens

See page 22.

The Small Breeds Farm Park & Owl Centre

See page 10.

Penrhos Gallery

See page 49.

Dunkertons Cider Mill & Restaurant

See page 16.

Border Trails

Explore the Marches at your own pace, by car, foot or bike, with a choice of trails. For further information ring Upper Newton Farmhouse, Kinnersley on 01544 327710.

September Dairy Products

See page 10.

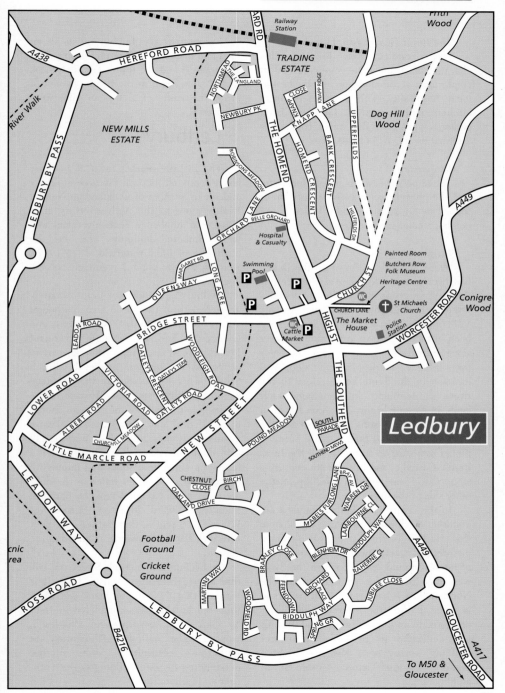

Ledbury

The Royal George Inn, Lyonshall

Just 3 miles from Kington, this charming black and white country inn offers comfortable accommodation and the best in local hospitality. This includes country kitchen and restaurant, lounge, bars, garden, real ales and fine wines. For further information ring 01544 340210.

Kinnersley

The imposing castle is mainly Jacobean, and the church has a 14th-century tower topped by an unusual gable. Inside is the notable Smalman monument.

Knighton

'Tref-y-clawdd' (the town on the Dyke), Knighton lies inside the Welsh border, at the halfway point on the 168-mile Offa's Dyke Path. The path was opened in July 1971 and walkers and school parties have been attracted here in great numbers ever since. So have the many visitors who enjoy this hillside market town's delightful location in the Teme Valley, close to the river's heavily-wooded and mountainous left bank. In its long history Knighton has been occupied by the Saxons, the Welsh and the Normans. The latter built a castle here – a timber structure on a mound still known as Bryn-y-Castell – and in the 12th century a stone castle was built on a hilltop on the other side of the town.

In the centre of Knighton stands a tall Victorian clock tower. Running uphill from this is The Narrows, the town's most picturesque street. There are also a number of interesting old inns, of which the Swan was once noted for cock fighting. The Norman church has been rebuilt twice and is one of the few churches in Wales dedicated to an English saint – and the only one dedicated to St Edward. Another building worthy of a visit is Knighton Station – a gem of Victorian-Gothic railway architecture.

Knighton is also famous for its sheep sales and market, which attract people from a wide area, and the town's fairs date back to 1230. In 1925, in the nearby hamlet of Stow, the ruins of a Roman villa were discovered.

Ledbury

The historic market town of Ledbury has a poetry all its own. Picturesque, lively and set in an Area of Outstanding Natural Beauty close to the Malvern Hills, it is home to a number of distinctive black and white timbered buildings and was the birthplace of John Masefield (1878-1967), who ran away to sea and eventually became Poet Laureate.

Ledbury is equidistant (approximately 15 miles) from the three great cathedral cities of Hereford, Worcester and Gloucester. And, interestingly, several of Ledbury's most fascinating attractions are to be found in cobbled, medieval Church Street. This takes you to the Heritage Centre and Butchers' Row Museum before climbing to the gates of the Norman church of St Michael and All Angels. The massive detached tower is 200 ft high and the tall spire dominates the skyline. The church is a feast of architectural styles and impressive monuments, and bullet holes in the door are a permanent reminder of the Battle of Ledbury. Edward Moulton Barrett (of Wimpole Street), the father of poet Elizabeth Barrett Browning, is buried at the church.

In Ledbury's wide High Street you will find the 17th-century Market Hall. It is believed that this striking black and white timbered building was completed in 1645 by John Abell, carpenter to Charles I. Opposite the hall is 14th-century St Katherine's Hospital, and another outstanding historic building is the 16th-century Feathers Hotel.

Ledbury

The town has a number of interesting visitor attractions, as described below, and is an excellent centre for shopping. In addition, the magnificent countryside surrounding Ledbury is home to hopyards, fruit orchards, cider makers and Herefordshire cattle. It is ideal walking country and the inspiration for several designated walks which include the Malvern Hills Trail, the Poet's Paths and the Dymock Daffodil Way. Details of these are available from Ledbury's Tourist Information Centre.

Elizabeth Barrett Browning Institute

A memorial to the author who spent her early years nearby, the building is now home to the town's library. It includes a collection of books associated with the Poets of Dymock and John Masefield, whose works are celebrated at the annual Ledbury Poetry Festival. For further information ring 01531 632133.

Butchers' Row House
See page 43.

Coddington Vineyard
See page 8.

Eastnor Castle
See page 18.

Guided walks around Ledbury

Throughout summer months you can step back in time along the Medieval Walk, or – if you dare – get into the spirit of old Ledbury on the infamous Ghost Walk. For further information ring 01531 634229.

Hellens
See page 19.

Ledbury Heritage Centre
See page 44.

Lyne Down Farm
See page 16.

Newbridge Farm Park
See page 9.

The Painted Room

Located above the town's council offices in Church Lane are unique 16th-century frescos. For opening times ring 01531 632306.

Three Choirs Vineyard
See page 10.

Westons Cider
See page 16.

Leintwardine

The hillside village of Leintwardine (pronounced Lentwardyne) stands at the north-western tip of the county, near the junction of the rivers Teme and Clun. It has suffered an unsettled and turbulent past: occupied by the Romans, then by the Saxons, raided by the Welsh and taken over by the Normans. The Roman road, Watling Street West – which runs through Herefordshire from north to south – crosses the River Teme here. The church dates from the 13th and 14th centuries and has a massive battlemented tower. General Tarleton, a cavalry leader who fought in the American War of Independence and died in the village in 1833, is buried here. Leintwardine has a pleasant village green and some interesting houses, and about three miles to the south-east is a delightful wooded gorge through which the Teme flows.

Leominster

An old market town of Saxon origins, Leominster stands at the junction of the rivers Pinsley and Lugg, fourteen miles due

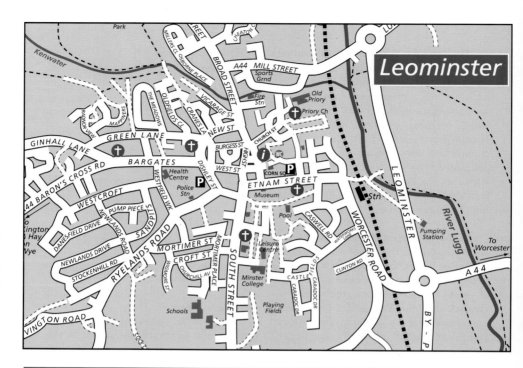

The Talbot Hotel
LEOMINSTER - HEREFORDSHIRE

A Coaching Inn originating from the 15th century.
Oak Beams, Log Fire & Traditional Hospitality.
All our comfortable bedrooms are en-suite and
have direct dial telephones, colour television,
tea/coffee making facilities,radio and a hair dryer.
A number have a trouser press. The hotel offers a
wide range of exelllent snacks and meals in the
lounge bars. Table d'hôte and a la carte menus are
presented to diners for lunch and dinner which is
served in the Berrington Restaurant.

**West Street, Leominster,
Herefordshire, HR6 8EP**
Reservations:
**Tel: 01568 616347
Fax: 01568 614880**

north of Hereford. This puts it within very easy reach of the county's unspoilt black and white villages of Eardisland, Eardisley, Pembridge and Weobley – but life here hasn't always been this peaceful. At the heart of the Marches, the area has witnessed a great deal of hostility, having been taken successively by the Welsh and the Danes before the English claimed it for Edward the Confessor. The most decisive battle of the first of the three Wars of the Roses took place at Mortimer's Cross, a few miles from Leominster, in February 1461.

Once prosperous for the superior quality of the wool produced by local Ryeland sheep, Leominster remains a busy market town and exports Hereford cattle all over the world. The town also retains many of its medieval and Tudor characteristics, including narrow streets, timber-framed buildings and the magnificent 12th-century Benedictine Priory, which is now the parish church. With such a distinguished heritage, it is appropriate that Leominster is also well established as one of the most important antique centres in the region. There are many shops, galleries and markets displaying a wide variety of antiques and collectables at prices starting from just a few pounds.

Leominster Festival in early June is one of the county's major cultural events. Some of the many other attractions in and near the town are described below.

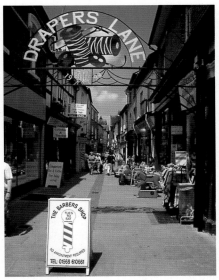

Leominster

The Grove Golf Centre & Hickory Stick Restaurant

This family attraction, set in thirty-five acres of beautiful Herefordshire countryside near Leominster, definitely believes in giving you a choice of main course! The superb golfing facilities include a 9-hole par 30 course, with many scenic features and hazards, as well as a covered and floodlit range, a 9-hole putting green, golf shop and professional tuition. Beginners and serious players alike are welcome, and there is no

stuffy dress code! The restaurant has balconies and views and occupies a fine old timber-framed building. Menus range from bar snacks to full a la carte. For further information and bookings (golf and/or restaurant) ring 01568 610602.

Historic buildings

Leominster's historic buildings include **Grange Court**, built in 1633 and moved to its present site in the 1850's; **Hester Clarke's Almhouses**, founded in 1735 and noted for its unusual decoration; **The Forbury**, a chapel of 1284 dedicated to Thomas a Becket and containing fine medieval roof timbers; **The Three Horseshoes**, an outstanding example of medieval domestic architecture; **Lion House**, formerly an important coaching inn and wagon centre; **Chequers Inn**, one of England's best examples of an early timber-framed inn and believed to date back to 1480; **The Old Priory Hospital**, originally part of the Benedictine Priory; and **Dutton House**, where the 1850 Gothic exterior fronts a house built in Tudor times.

Leominster

Leominster Folk Museum
See page 44.

Leominster Leisure Centre
There is something here for everyone – a large sports hall, dance studio, squash courts, weight training, aerobic classes, lifestyle fitness testing and much more. For further information ring 01568 615578.

Lion Gallery
See page 47.

Priory Church
See page 34.

Queenswood Country Park
See page 26.

Lingen
Close to the Welsh border in the lovely countryside of remote north-west Herefordshire, Lingen is a quiet and pleasant village. There are numerous half-timbered cottages in the main street and good views from the castle mound, near to the church. About a mile to the south-east are the scant remains of Limebrook Priory in the beautiful Lugg Valley.

Leominster - Priory Church

Longtown

Longtown's attraction is the ruined round keep of the 12th-century castle, now in the care of English Heritage. A gallows stood on the castle mound, and the last time a murderer was hanged here was in the 18th century.

Lucton

A village of black and white cottages, Lucton is also notable for two other buildings: the school, which has a charming facade built in 1708, and Lucton Mill, dating from the 18th century and working up until 1940.

Madley

About six miles west of Hereford, between the River Wye and the Black Mountains, Madley is another charming village of half-timbered houses. But undoubtedly its biggest attraction is the church. Built in the 13th and 14th centuries of local sandstone, it boasts one of the largest medieval fonts in Britain and 13th-century stained glass. See also page 34.

Mansel Lacy

A few miles north-west of Hereford, off the A480, the village stands at the entrance to the Foxley Estate, which was once the home of Sir Uvedale Price (1747-1829), a leading exponent of the picturesque landscaping movement. The former post office has a dovecote in its gabled end.

Marden

The village stands on the River Lugg between Hereford and Leominster. The church, dating mainly from the 14th century, has an open well which some experts believe marks the site where St Ethelbert was murdered in c794.

Michaelchurch Escley

Lying close to the Golden Valley,

Monmouth

between the River Dore and the Black Mountains, the village's main claim to fame is its church. Dedicated to St Michael, it has a rare wall painting on its north wall, created in about 1500.

Monmouth

A thriving market town on the Welsh border, south-west of Ross-on-Wye, Monmouth has narrow winding medieval streets and a proliferation of well-preserved Tudor and Georgian buildings. Henry V was born in Monmouth Castle, now a ruin, in 1387, and he is remembered in a statue overlooking Agincourt Square in the very centre of the town.

There are many fine buildings in Monmouth, including the 18th-century Shire Hall, 17th-century Great Castle House and St Mary's church, which was

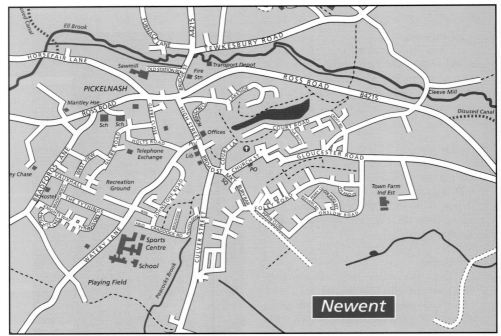

Newent

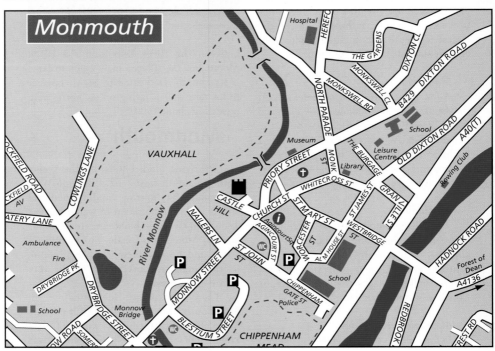

Monmouth

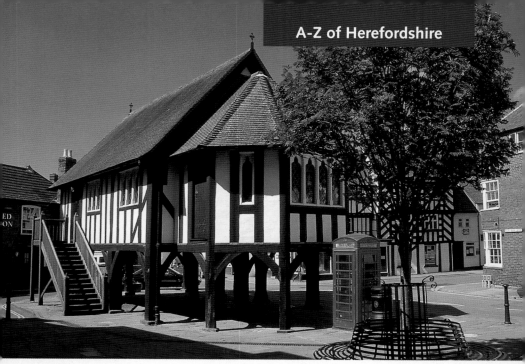

Newent

founded in Norman times. The great spire is nearly 200 feet high and presents an unmissable landmark from whichever direction you approach the town. Spanning the river at the bottom of Monnow Street is the 13th-century gated Monnow Bridge, built originally as a defensive measure and one of very few structures of its type left in Europe.

Two miles east of Monmouth, on the opposite side of the Wye Valley, is Kymin Hill, which on a clear day gives spectacular views over the surrounding countryside.

Mordiford

Mordiford, on the River Lugg, has a place in Herefordshire legend. The Mordiford Dragon was said to descend from the hills to feed on local maidens, until it was killed by a criminal who also died in the fight. Prior to the building of the church tower in 1811, the west gable of the church featured a 12-foot figure of this fearsome monster. A more terrifying reality was the flood which once roared down the valley with fatal consequences – a disaster which explains the height of the flood defences on the Lugg. Ancient cottages decorate the winding village street, and other interesting features include the Georgian rectory and the 14th-century bridge.

Mortimer's Cross

This hamlet 8 miles north-west of Leominster was the site of a particularly bloody and decisive battle in 1461 during the first of the Wars of the Roses. See page 102 (*Wigmore*).

Much Marcle

Lying in Big Apple country 7 miles north-east of Ross-on-Wye, the village of Much Marcle played an important role in the development of the cidermaking industry in Herefordshire. In the 19th century a local farmer, Henry Weston, was one of the first men to start a cider factory, and the company he established is today a

Ross-on-Wye

thriving business. The church, built between the 13th and 15th centuries, contains a series of interesting monuments – some of the finest carved effigies in the county.

Hellens
See page 19.

Lyne Down Farm
See page 16.

Westons Cider
See page 16.

Newent
A pleasant and attractive Gloucestershire border town, Newent was the birthplace of Dick Whittington, who became Lord Mayor of London three times.

A unique attraction today is The Shambles, a recreation of a Victorian village complete with shops and other authentic buildings. Just outside the town are the National Birds of Prey Centre and The Three Choirs Vineyard.

Orleton
A village of black and white houses, this is the home of 16th-century Orleton Court, where Charles I reputedly stayed in 1645 and Alexander Pope was a later visitor. The church has a fine Norman font and a timber porch built in 1686.

Pembridge
See page 38.

Peterchurch
Peterchurch is the centre for the

THE JUDGE'S LODGING
Presteigne, Powys.

LLETY'R BARNWR

THE JUDGE'S · LODGING ·

Winner of 'Interpret Britain' Award 1998
and
'Britain's Local Museum of the Year' 1999

Explore the 'upstairs, downstairs' life of the
Victorian judges, their servants and felonious guests
at this stunningly restored 'hands-on' historic house

Plus...
Courtroom,
Audio Tour
featuring Robert
Hardy, Local
History Rooms,
Tourist Information
Centre, Shop.

Open daily 10am - 6pm
1st March - 31st October Winter opening may vary, so please call.
Broad Street, Presteigne, Powys LD8 2AD
Telephone enquiries 01544 260650 ● www.judgeslodging.org.uk

Golden Valley and has an interesting Norman church, as described on page 34.

Presteigne

A small Welsh border town on the west bank of the River Lugg, Presteigne grew up around a Norman castle, nothing of which survives. Fine Georgian houses can be seen in Broad Street, but one of the town's most striking buildings is the half-timbered Radnorshire Arms Hotel, built as a private house in 1606 and boasting several interesting features. Among the town's major visitor attractions are the Judge's Lodgings – formerly the Shire Hall – and Bryan's Ground, an Edwardian garden under restoration in the Lugg Valley.

Ross-on-Wye

If you're planning on touring the Wye Valley, you won't a better base than the lovely market town of Ross. It is proudly perched on a high sandstone bluff overlooking a loop of the river known as Horseshoe Bend, and is a magnet for shoppers and tourists. The town walls, although medieval in appearance, were built in the 1830's to help attract new prosperity and establish Ross as an important holiday and resort town.

In the centre is the 17th-century Market Housel, constructed of red sandstone and now home to the town's Heritage Centre. Opposite stands the house of John Kyrle (1637-1725) – 'the man of Ross'. He was responsible for installing the town's first water supply, as well as constructing a causeway from Wilton Bridge and laying out the Prospect Gardens.

Another striking feature of Ross is the famous spire of St Mary's church. Towering more than sixty metres in height, it is visible for miles around.

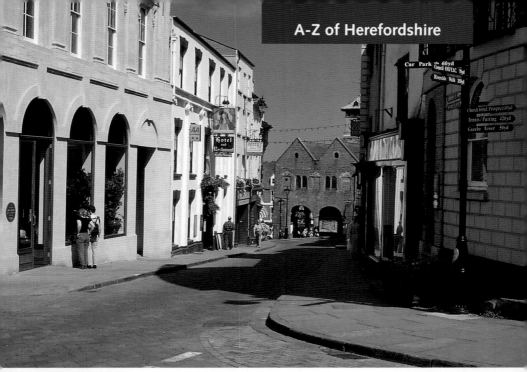

Ross-on-Wye

The town's beautiful riverside setting provides the perfect venue for a host of annual events, including the Ross-on-Wye Regatta and the 100-mile Raft Race, and this is also a major centre for sporting and leisure activities – everything from angling, canoeing, cycling and ballooning to swimming, tennis and skateboarding.

South-west of Ross-on-Wye, close to Monmouth, is the famous beauty spot of Symonds Yat. From here to Chepstow the Wye cuts a spectacular course through dramatic gorge scenery. And also south of Ross, stretching between the Wye and the Severn, is the vast expanse of the Royal Forest of Dean.

Other visitor attractions are described briefly below.

Cloisters Restaurant

This charming little restaurant and wine bar in Ross-on-Wye specialises in fish dishes. For further information and

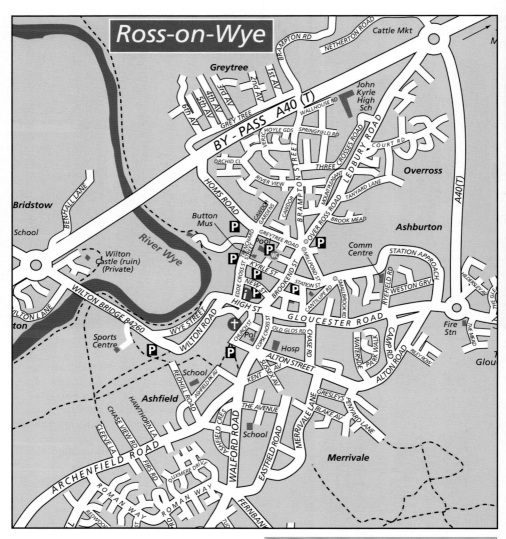

reservations ring 01989 567717.

Goodrich Castle
See page 19.

Le Faisan Dore Brasserie
Formerly known as Pheasants Restaurant, Le Faisan Dore Brasserie in Ross-on-Wye is a restaurant with international character. Chef and patronne Eileen Brunnarius, a member of the

prestigious Master Chefs of Great Britain, uses local ingredients wherever possible and offers a range of dishes to suit most palates at reasonable prices. For further information ring 01989 565761.

Market House Heritage Centre
See page 44.

Prospect Gardens
These provide panoramic views over the River Wye.

The Royal Forest of Dean
The forest covers 27,000 acres and is a mixed woodland of broadleaf trees and conifers. At the western edge of the forest lies the River Wye, while the eastern border reaches the River Severn.

St Mary's Church
See page 34.

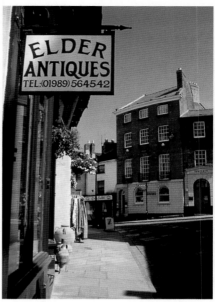

Ross-on-Wye

South Herefordshire Golf Club

Located at Upton Bishop, just 5 minutes' drive from Ross-on-Wye and only 3 miles from the M50, the club has a 16-bay all-weather driving range, a 9-hole Academy Course for beginners and a challenging 18-hole course for more experienced players. 3-day and 5-day golfing holiday packages are also available For further information ring 01989 780535.

Weather Station

Located close to the churchyard of St Mary's, the station permits you (by prior arrangement) to see the weather monitoring instruments in use.

Shobdon

Just a few miles from Leominster in the north-west of the county, Shobdon is a village with several interesting features. The church, built in the middle of the 18th century on an adjoining 12th-century Norman tower, has a striking Georgian Gothic interior – said to be one of the finest examples of its kind in England. Also surviving from the church's medieval predecessor are renovated Shobdon Arches, rebuilt on their present site nearby.

Another attraction for visitors is the giant sessile oak tree which stands opposite Easthampton Farm. Reputedly the largest in the country and several centuries old, it is 32 feet in circumference, weighs approximately 80 tonnes and produces an estimated 8 million leaves every year! For a bird's-eye view of the tree you can make the short trip to Shobdon airfield, which is now a major centre for flying training, gliding and microlighting. An air race and the village carnival are just of the two annual events held in Shobdon in summer months. The Visitor Centre close to the church has full details, along with a wealth of other local information.

Rural Herefordshire

St Margaret's

See page 35.

Staunton-on-Wye

Lying between the Forest of Dean national forest park and the Wye Valley, Staunton has a Norman to Perpendicular church which contains two fonts – one Norman and one of later decorated style. The Buck Stone provides a dramatic viewpoint at its lofty elevation of 900ft.

Stretton Sugwas

Located on the western outskirts of Hereford, on the Brecon road, the village of Stretton Sugwas has an interesting church. Its features include a black and white timbered tower and three Norman doorways, over one of which is a remarkable preserved carved tympanum. Also of note is an engraved stone dated 1473.

Symonds Yat

Symonds Yat

A famous beauty spot lying in a narrow loop of the Wye, Symonds Yat is only a short distance from the town of Ross and the castle village of Goodrich. From the summit of Yat Rock (473ft), which is accessible by road on the Gloucestershire side, the views are magnificent as the river winds through a richly-wooded setting. On the same side of the Wye are picturesque Coldwell Rocks.

Tarrington

Midway between Hereford and Ledbury (approximately 7 miles from each), the village is home to The Millpond – an attractive and popular site for anglers, touring caravanners and campers. The water is well stocked with mixed coarse fish, and alongside are toilets, showers, electric hitch-ups, hot and cold water, shaver points, telephone and disabled facilities. For further information and bookings ring 01432 890243.

Tenbury Wells

A market town in the Teme Valley, Tenbury Wells sits just inside the Worcestershire border to the north-east of Leominster. Once a prosperous spa town well patronised by the Victorians for its medicinal saline spring waters, Tenbury has attractive old black and white houses and its share of other interesting buildings. Amongst them is the restored Victorian Pump Room,

the 18th-century church with its 12th-century tower, and Burford House, built in the early 18th century just across the river from the town. There is also a round Market House, still in weekly use and the venue for the December holly and mistletoe markets – the largest in the country. Tenbury Wells is an ideal base for exploring the tranquil Teme Valley, an extensive area of hops and orchards.

Vowchurch

Located in the Golden Valley, this quiet village is interesting for the display of fine Jacobean woodwork in the church, including a superbly turned and carved wooden porch.

Weobley

See page 42.

Weston-under-Penyard

A hillside village two miles east of Ross-on-Wye, Weston dates back to the Romans. They founded it as a garrison town and used it to smelt the iron ore they extracted from the Forest of Dean. Virtually nothing remains of medieval Penyard Castle, but other buildings of interest in or near the village include the houses of Lower Weston and Bollitree Castle and St Lawrence church, which has four Norman arches and a 14th-century bell tower.

Wigmore

The north Herefordshire village of Wigmore is known for its associations with the Mortimer family – the most powerful of the Norman Marcher lords. Edward IV, a descendant of the family, became king by virtue of his victory in the Battle of Mortimer's Cross (1461), which was one of the most decisive confrontations in the Wars of the Roses.

Extensive Wigmore Castle, dating back to the 12th century, was the Mortimers' fortified palace, suffering the fate of many castles during the Civil War when it was pulled down by Cromwell's troops to prevent it falling into Royalist hands. It is now the subject of a restoration project by English Heritage and is not open to visitors.

The history of the village, which became a Norman borough, can be traced along a prescribed trail. Close to the castle is St. James's, a large early Norman church which has several notable features, such as Saxon herringbone masonry in the north wall.

The area surrounding Wigmore is wonderful walking and cycling country, and the village's variety of attractive accommodation includes opportunities to stay in some of Wigmore's most historic houses.

Woolhope

Located to the east of Hereford, this quiet village with its Norman to 14th-century church and old cottages stands in an area known as the Woolhope Dome – a curious natural phenomenon of great interest to geologists, so called because the low wooded hills rise beside the River Wye in a series of concentric ridges and valleys.

Yarpole

This attractive village lies to the north of Leominster, not far from Croft Castle and Croft Ambrey Iron Age camp. The church, thought to be of 14th-century origin, is one of the seven churches of Herefordshire with a detached bell tower. Another unusual building is the timbered medieval gatehouse which stands on the bank of a stream in the centre of the village.

Index

A
Abbey Dore 6, 22, 31, 63
Allensmore 31
Almeley 63
Arthur's Stone 17
arts & crafts 47-49

B
Bacton 63
Ballingham 63
Barrett Browning, Elizabeth 82, 85
Berrington Hall 17
Bishop's Frome 31, 47, 66
Black & White Villages 37-42
Black & White Village Trail 37
Blakemere 66
Bockleton 66
Bodenham 66
Bosbury 66
Brampton Abbots 31
Brampton Bryan 66
Bredwardine 31, 67
British Camp 9
Brockhampton 32, 67
Bromyard 32, 43, 46, 48, 68

C
Capler Camp 17
Castle Frome 72
churches & cathedrals 29-35
cider 11-16
Clifford Castle 17, 21
Clodock 72
Clyro 47
Coleford 72
Colwall 72
Cradley 72
Craswall 74
Croft Ambrey 17
Croft Castle 18
cycleways 8

D
Dilwyn 37
Dinedor Camp 18
Dorstone 6, 74

E
Eardisland 28, 32, 37, 43
Eardisley 38
Eastnor 48, 74
Eastnor Castle 18
Eaton Bishop 32
Elgar, Edward 9
Eyton 74

F
Fownhope 32, 74
Foy 32

G
gardens 22-28
Garway 74
Golden Valley 6
Goodrich 32, 75
Goodrich Castle 19
Great Malvern 9, 75

H
Hay-on-Wye 75, 76
Hereford 7, 33, 43, 44, 46, 49-62
Hereford Cathedral 33, 57, 58, 59
Herefordshire 5-7
Herefordshire Beacon 9, 21
Herefordshire Cider Route 12
Hidden Highway 8
historic houses 17-21
Hoarwithy 77
Holme Lacy 77
Hope-under-Dinmore 77
Hop Trail 9
How Caple 33

K
Kilpeck 33, 78
Kilvert, Francis 31, 47, 67, 76
Kingsland 79
Kinnersley 82
King's Caple 79
Kington 33, 44, 47, 49, 79, 80
Knighton 82

L
Ledbury 8, 34, 43, 44, 47, 82-83
Leintwardine 34, 85
Leominster 7, 34, 44, 47, 48, 87-88
Lingen 88
Longtown 89
Loughton Castle 21
Lower Brockhampton 21
Lucton 89
Lyonshall 35, 82

M
Madley 34, 89
Malvern Hills 9
Mansel Lacy 89
Mappa Mundi & Chained Library 54, 57, 58
Marden 89
Masefield, John 82, 85
Michaelchurch Escley 89
Monmouth 89, 91
Mordiford 91
Mortimer's Cross 91
Mortimer Trail 10
Much Marcle 91
museums & heritage centres 43-46

N
Newent 45, 91, 92

O
Offa, King 6, 50
Offa's Dyke 6
Offa's Dyke Path 6, 10
Orleton 92

P
parks & gardens 22-28
Pembridge 34, 38-41, 48
Peterchurch 34, 92
picnic sites 9
Presteigne 44, 94

Q
Queensway Country Park 26

R
Ross-on-Wye 7, 8, 34, 44, 45, 48, 92, 94-99
Rowlstone 35
Royal Forest of Dean 7, 97

S
Shobdon 35, 99
Snodhill Castle 6, 21
Staunton-on-Wye 100
St Margaret's 35
Stretton Sugwas 100
Symonds Yat 100, 101
Symonds Yat Rock 7

T
Tarrington 101
Tenbury Wells 101, 102

U
Upton Bishop 49

V
Vowchurch 74, 102

W
Walford 35
walking 10
Weobley 42, 46
Weston-under-Penyard 102
Wigmore 102
Woolhope 102
Wormelow 46
Wye Valley 7
Wye Valley Walk 10

Y
Yarpole 103